PEARLS ON I

… Dedicated to all those
treasured individuals within
these pages … to those not
here but still being held in my
heart, for the PEARLS
that you are and the pearls
that you have shown me.

Thank you!

WHY "PEARLS"?

Pearl was my grandmother's name.

Her given name was Mabel Priscilla, but the characters that make up my family rarely use their full, given names. I come from a line of rugged individualists.

Elizabeth Louise (known as Beth). George Macmillan (known as Mac). I am Cynthia Louise (known as Cinder) ... you get the idea.

As life has unfolded for me, there have been moments of clarity, of significant JOY, and sometimes of lessons that have challenged, tormented, or pushed me to my limits ... which then eventually become pearls of wisdom. I believe it is important to deeply recognize, celebrate, and be willing to make use of and even share those pearls.

That is what I've set out to do in this collection of poems, stories, and reflections on the pearls I've strung together in my life. I hope to give my readers bits of information about sustaining the appreciation of life's gifts to maintain an attitude of gratitude through the string that stretches out between the pearls.

I am grateful to the Earth-bound and the archetypal supporters who have helped me enjoy my string of pearls as the gifts they are.

GRIT

That's what they say it takes to form a pearl. A bit of grit buried deep within a shell containing muck, flushed with sand, incubated in time, deep under the sea.

I was born in June of 1955, a bit early for full ripening; though, apparently my mom had had enough of me, and it was time to make an appearance in the world. I was born by cesarean section, plucked out of a warm if somewhat unsettled belly and thrust into the cold sterility of a hospital environment.

Although rumour has it my mom welcomed the idea of another child, the experience of bringing me into the world was evidently a fearful and threatening one. I'm not at all sure I've been forgiven yet. From the stories told, my mom probably experienced after my birth what would today be labelled "postpartum depression." Nerve problems that we might characterize as panic attacks and general malaise were an issue.

Mom had a successful career with a large cosmetics and pharmaceutical company before she married my dad. The image of my mom going door to door in her early career with that company, singing their jingle and challenging the homeowner to identify the tune, always amused me as a child. An accurate sense of pitch and vocal control did not seem to be one of her strong points.

Once married, following my dad's wishes, she tried to stay home with the babies. Probably, that added to her discomfort.

Finally, in 1957, she went to work with Dad at the golf club he was operating, selling liquor tickets for a banquet being held one night. As Dad used to say, "She never really went home."

Being the child of two working parents (years before that became the social norm) meant that, for most of my childhood, there was a live-in babysitter for my older brother, Robbie, and me in the bungalow where we lived on the driveway to the golf club. For most of each year, our lives revolved around the club. Many of the members were very kind to me.

At times, it was like having hundreds of extended family, who listened to my stories, told me jokes, and encouraged me in the game of golf. There were many golden moments. The Saturday night dances were an opportunity to peek out from behind the kitchen doors, watching members ballroom-dancing to the music of the Johnny Linden Orchestra. I loved to listen to my dad singing "Mac the Knife" with the band.

I followed my dad around like a puppy much of the time, whether he was setting up the bar, plowing snow, or putting out the sprinklers late at night. We both enjoyed word play, and he regularly had a joke or shaggy-dog story to share. He always had a way to get me laughing. Mom took work hours much more seriously, and to spend time with her during the day meant learning how to do various jobs at the club, whether it was adding up member accounts on the adding machine in the office or using the floor polisher on the banquet hall's parquet flooring. It all worked well enough in day-to-day life as a younger child.

As a teenager, I had a harder time with our relationship (or lack thereof). As a young teen, I could relate to the old Smothers Brothers' routine: "Mom always loved YOU best!" The preferred sibling, in my mind, was her work at the club.

At 14 years of age, I was diagnosed with type 1 diabetes. Once the ensuing panic subsided a bit, Mom took this on like a work mission. All my food was weighed and portioned out with military precision. I remember that such things as sleepovers, which other young girls at school seemed to enjoy, were out of the question.

She did encourage, and in fact took on a leadership role in, 4-H courses locally, which I did enjoy. But it became obvious to me that being in control of the situation was the main factor in her decisions about what I was allowed to do. One way or another, it became clear to me that diabetes was seen not so much as my challenge but her burden.

As a child, and certainly as a teen, I do not remember physical affection being expressed between me and my mom. The only real contact was a controlling hand on my collarbone in my younger years. Since I grew taller than my mom, it would have been awkward for her to try to exert physical control. A vague sense of disappointment and guilt, along with (at that stage) a lack of recognition of individual worth, was enough of a control device. But, it didn't always work as she intended. I became inwardly rebellious, though limited in my ways of expressing that rebellion.

Mom's version of parental concern was simply to worry actively and suffer a great deal, rather than anything that could be construed as a recognizable sign of affection. The word "love" was taboo, and I always had the feeling that I was not living up to her expectations of me.

Looking back, I can recognize, on an emotional level, a sort of triangular relationship between my mom, my dad, and me. Dad and I shared a sense of humour, love of music, and enjoyment of golf, which was all carried out with an over-arching caution so as not to upset Mother. My mom had little patience for our shenanigans. She may well have been feeling like the workhorse of the family and largely left out of the fun. It's not that she lacked a sense of humour or an ability to tell stories and laugh, she just didn't share an affinity for the same kind of silliness that we shared.

Various things said over the years indicated she was a bit resentful of the closeness Dad and I shared, and our perceived lack of respect for her attempts to manage our behaviour. She would attack her duties with a passion. She was able to prepare exceptional meals, decorate the house or clubhouse beautifully, balance the books to the penny, and learn new skills quickly and eagerly, setting very high standards for herself in each case. Mom would attend functions and support our school in any way she could, all the while micromanaging the office and other duties in the golf course clubhouse with a determination rarely seen and thus admired by those who appreciated correctness. Mom was heroic in her style and her intentions.

One story that illustrates her emphasis on keeping unquestionably correct records happened in the 1960s.

A tax audit was conducted on the books from the golf business. At the time, she was still doing the bookkeeping in a home office in our bungalow, which sat the length of the parking lot away from the clubhouse. The club had a banquet scheduled that same day, and she was very busy preparing for it. Dad stayed at the house in case the auditor needed anything, and Mom went to prepare for the event. The auditor found what he considered an irregularity in the ledgers at the house that Dad wasn't able to explain. The auditor declared that he required an answer before he could finish the audit.

Reluctantly, Dad went over to the club and let Mom know the auditor needed to see her about something he'd found wrong in the books. Skeptical and disgruntled that the auditor thought she had an error in her records, she marched, oven mitts still on her hands, across the parking lot to the house and down to the office in the basement.

Upon entering the office, she demanded, "What's the matter with you? I'm BUSY!!"

The auditor cleared his throat and said, "Madam, there is an item listed as Chicken Festival entered as a maintenance expense in your ledger. Can you explain that please? It should be under the revenue column, I would think."

She stared at him, wide-eyed, and asked, "What's the dollar amount?"

"Two thousand dollars" came the reply.

"Oh, for heaven's sake!" she cried. "That's chicken shit!"

The auditor sat up a little straighter and said, "Madam, your government does not consider two thousand dollars to be chicken shit."

"I know that!" she sputtered. Then, pointing at Dad, she said, "His father would buy ANYTHING if he was convinced it was a bargain! It's in a pile on the south field if you think you need to go and have a look at it. Now, do you think I could go back over and get back to doing something USEFUL?"

It was quite a while before she was audited again.

Dad would defend her to outside judges or those who didn't respect her dictates, but if an opportunity came up for a bit of fun, he was not above teasing her about her rather unusual version of diplomacy.

My brother, Rob, and I had very different modes of coping with the mixed messages of our childhood. Once he hit the teen years, Rob learned to act out. I just learned to act.

Rob was a volatile bundle of need-for-attention. For much of our childhood/teen years, I was afraid of him. Once angered, he seemed out of control, and I feared his anger would result in real harm to me.

For my part, I was a terrible irritant to him. Rob was older, bigger, and very strong physically compared to me. I was quicker with sarcasm and would taunt him by out-performing him in school and avoiding trouble with the authorities; whereas, he seemed to land in trouble all the time!

My relationship with my brother was at times diffi-cult, especially in response to the pressures we each felt about controlling parents and lack of affection or respect. Despite remarkable efforts on Dad's part to bridge the distance, Rob and Mom were both quick to anger and explosive in their expression of anger, though it faded quickly once the incident was over.

I think it's fair to say that both Dad and I had longer fuses and were slow to anger. I don't think either of us was particularly comfortable with the conflict and anger liable to break out at any given moment ... and that it never really seemed to be far away.

CAT-O-NINE

Cat-o-nine tails
there you sit
prickly cranky
ready to
scratch a hole
gut-deep.

Predator
where did you get
the strength
to render me
a victim,
restrained,
as if to move
would be to risk
abrasion.

If I were
to take
your power
de-claw you
like a house cat
domesticate
and tame you,
would you learn to mind
or undermine
my efforts
to make peace.

If I were
determined in
my efforts

to dislodge you,
would you rip and
tear a passage
or disintegrate
like kidney stones
that lasers shatter,
ultrasounds
recording
their destruction
and if I were
successful
in extracting you,
what creature then
would move to fill
the space
that you now occupy.

Cat-o-nine
ours is a
fearful
synergy.

THE COMFORT OF TREES

Throughout my life, trees have provided me with profound comfort. As a child, I was very fortunate to have a forest between our yard and the valley next to us. That forest was a place of safety. When my emotions got the better of me and I was close to an outburst, which would NOT have been acceptable at home, I would scoot as quickly as possible into the trees. Not far away, but in what felt like a completely different world.

I can still see myself leaning up against a tree, puzzling over a conundrum, and waiting for the wisdom of the tree to clarify things for me. Each type of tree seemed to have its own language. Some, like my favourite apple tree, simply provided a sense of personal space for contemplation. Willow trees provided flexible, long twigs from which Anchie (our nanny) taught me how to weave wicker-like miniature furniture to play with. I'd set up little homes I'd imagine living in.

One time, when I was bedridden with a nasty case of strep throat, there came a knock at my window. I peered out through foggy eyes to see Mom's hand holding a baby rabbit for me to look at. A nest of bunnies had taken up residence between the roots of a giant old oak.

Once a year, on or around my birthday, my grandmother used to walk with me out to the end of our yard. We followed a path that wound its way through the forest to a particularly straight, clear trunk. She would take a flat stone and very carefully mark my height, scraping a little line into the wood of the tree.

Only years later did I notice that the tree itself never seemed to get any taller. Amused by my observation, Grandma just grinned wryly and pointed upward. I looked UP ... w-a-a-ay UP ... and for the first time, realized that the tree was actually a utility pole at the edge of the slope leading down to the road. We shared a laugh over that one!

It was another place in the forest, though, that I visited when emotions ran high in my girlhood. Looking back, I'd say this special little sanctuary was my first holy place where I could retreat and safely allow myself to simply BE.

There was no judgement or rancour to be dealt with in my little nook made up of the lower branches of several trees. The floor was mossy. The branches aromatic, as only pines can be.

There was even, conveniently enough, a cinder block on the floor of that green cave. I never spent time wondering about who might have put it there. Somehow, the rule came into my mind that the forest would tell me when it was calm and safe to return home. The signal would be a snail, crawling across my view ... he always did. Eventually.

FOREST NOOK

Branches of the giant trees
enclosed with graceful curving arms
a nook my soul can go to
when my emotions sound alarms.

Bare feet feeling the emerald moss
squishing soft beneath my toes
perched upon the cinder block
till the vessel overflows.

This is the place of refuge, peace,
a place to hum, a place to wail
a place to feel myself restored
while waiting for a snail ...

MYTHING LINKS: SPRINKLERS

The warm breeze tickles your face and lifts your hair away from your ears, as though you are about to take flight. Close your eyes and inhale the sweet smell of wet grass. All is well in your world.

Dad is driving the old pickup truck with its worn tires through the star-filled night to the next hole on the golf course. Right on cue, you hop down from the truck, sprinkler in hand, to fasten it into its connection then spring back up onto the tailgate, time after time, until everything is in place.

Over at the edge of the pond, Dad turns the big wheel that lets the water go. You listen intently for the sound *cushshshsh ... chik ... chik ... chik ...* which means you've done your job well. The watering of the course is underway for the night.

"C'mon, McNut," says Dad. "Time to get you home to bed."

Magical nights like this are all part of the adventures to be enjoyed as a child of a golf course builder and operator like my dad. That magical sense of serenity and lush sensual pleasure still fills my soul when I spend time on a golf course. Opportunities may present themselves in the course of my work as a golf club manager or while out enjoying a game with my golfing buddies. (On a golf course, for those who don't play, a "buddy" is defined as a player in your foursome regularly, who understands that, on a golf course, a little verbal abuse is a sign of affection.)

As a golfer, it is the times when that sense of serenity is with me that I play at my best. I have reached the following conclusion … are you ready for it? Golf is a Zen thing; it is NOT technical wizardry.

Oh, the club manufacturers might tell you otherwise. The fellows who seem to be out there in the game mostly for the purpose of developing ulcers, will tell you otherwise. Even the nasty little voice in your mind that loves to rhyme off all sorts of personal faults and technical errors in your swing may tell you otherwise.

Have you ever noticed, though, when you watch the players on tour, that the most successful players are the same ones who enjoy the most smiles and chuckles out there? Now, you might say they are smiling because they're making more money than the other players. I would argue they are making more money *because* they are having more fun.

The love of the game. It's the only worthwhile reason to be on a golf course.

Well … along with the smell of wet, fresh cut grass and the breeze tickling your face, lifting your hair away from your ears …

THE DEER

branches,

their arms entwined

like Celtic knots

in a flowing rhythm dance with each other

meadow grasses gently stretching

up to greet the sun

welcome beauty

in the stance of a deer

gazing into awareness

with the eyes of a goddess

far above, a plump and satisfied bird

watches smugly from a high branch

comfortable with the miracle of knowing

that any time he chooses

he can take to the sky ...

ARE YOU LEAVING SO SOON?

One dark, early morning in the spring of 1975, I sat looking out the high-rise window of a friend's apartment in North York. The phone rang in the kitchen. I glanced at my watch wondering who would be calling at such an early hour. Rather than have it wake up my friends, I went to answer the phone.

A man's familiar, resonant voice identified himself in a rather proper, almost military tone and stated he was trying to locate and contact Cynthia Frost (my maiden name).

He was going to continue talking, but I cut him off, blurting out, "Uncle Bob. It's me!"

That seemed to catch him off guard. I don't think he was expecting that I would be the one answering the phone. I no longer lived at the address because I had gone off to university. My former roommate still lived there, though, and I was in town for a visit. I was 19 years old at the time. Somewhat tentatively I asked him, "Is something wrong, Uncle Bob?"

Uncle Bob was not really a blood relative, but he and my dad had been close friends since their school days in Toronto. Uncle Bob and his family had been like an extended family to us all my life. He met his wife, Trudy, when she was working for my parents as a newly immigrated nanny. She would often (joking of course) give me credit for introducing them when I was just a baby riding around on her hip.

I could hear Trudy's voice in the background as Uncle Bob cleared his throat and answered. My brother, Robbie, had been in an accident and was in the hospital in Scarborough.

I assumed he meant a car accident and asked, "Had he been drinking or anything?" Uncle Bob didn't know. He asked if I had a car at my apartment. I didn't, but I told him I was sure one of my friends would lend me theirs.

"Which hospital?" In the background, I could hear Aunt Trudy protesting. When Uncle Bob came back on the line, he asked where I was. After getting directions, he said, "Your Aunt Trudy and I will come and pick you up."

I said, "Thank you," and hung up the phone. My friends had woken up and were gathered in the room, looking at me with a question in their eyes.

I looked at them and, keeping my voice matter-of-fact, said, "That was my Uncle Bob. Rob has been in an accident, and they're coming to pick me up. I think he's dead. I'd better pack a toothbrush or something. I don't know how long I'll be."

Everyone was silenced by that statement.

A little shocked, they set about helping me get ready to go. I took my overnight kit and went downstairs to wait at the entrance.

Before long, a big, familiar navy blue car pulled up to the door. My Aunt Trudy got out of the car and pulled me to her ample bosom. A long, strong hug followed, and then I knew for sure. My brother was dead.

We climbed into the back seat, Trudy and I, and she held me close while I asked questions about what had happened.

For the past several years, Rob had been a snow-mobile racer with the Ontario Snowmobile Racing Federation. He had amassed a trunk full of trophies and ribbons for his wins on the tracks. His day job (or perhaps I should say his night job) was as manager of a bar/dance club in downtown Toronto.

Apparently, he had invited his staff and co-workers to party at my parents' home near Scarborough while they were away on a trip to Florida. The racing machines were kept in a barn out back.

It was dark out. Most of the snow was gone, with just a skiff on the ground. That did not deter his friends from pestering him to show them the racing machine he'd been bragging about at work. They even got the machine out of the barn and pulled it up to the back door.

Still dressed in business suits, Rob and his good friend Ron (with whom he shared an apartment) got onto the machine and rode off to take it for a spin around the sod field next to the house. They were gone longer than expected so some of the guests went out into the night to look for them.

They were discovered in the sod field, with no sign of life, either of them. A forensic investigation found that the throttle of the machine had stuck open at full speed. They were making a path with long corners around the field. I suspect Robbie was hoping they would run out of gas, since the racing machine had a relatively small gas tank. It would have been his best hope, since they couldn't slow down.

[Rob's School Photo *1971*]

They hit a bump in the field, were tossed up in the air, and both young men and the machine fell back to the ground. The police were called. They contacted Uncle Bob when they found his business card in Rob's wallet.

When Mom was trying to get her thoughts in order for the funeral arrangements, she asked me if Rob had ever told me anything about what he'd like at his funeral. Searching my mind for a clue, I remembered him saying he liked yellow roses. I don't think we were actually talking about funerals at the time, but looking at Mom's face, seeing her need to find something he'd like, I thought it would do.

So "yellow roses" was my answer, and she ordered a spray of yellow roses for his casket. The next morning, a family friend, on hearing of Rob's death, without any telephone or other conversation having sparked it, sent a bouquet of-you guessed it-yellow roses.

Later in the day, I asked my parents if I could go back to the apartment where Uncle Bob had found me the weekend before. I could serve no purpose at home and wanted to be with my friends, whom I'd left kind of hanging.

I went over for the evening; about six of my friends were gathered there. All were very sympathetic and supportive, and I appreciated their company. I had a guitar at the apartment and offered to sing them a song called "Robbie, hey Robbie" that I'd written in the past few days.

I sang my song for them, and as I finished, one of my friends, Doug, gently patted the back of my neck, tugging on my hair in a gesture of caring. That gesture was identical in energy and style to one my brother would use to express affection. I was sure it was Rob communicating through Doug.

One night, while I was still staying at the house and before I went back to university, I woke up in my old bedroom to see Rob standing near my closet looking down on me. I was wide awake then!

I spoke to him, saying, "Rob, I'm glad you're okay, but you're scaring the crap out of me! Please don't just show up like this. I can't handle it right now!" It was years before he made another appearance.

Years later, almost 20 years, in fact, I experienced him another time. I was receiving a Reiki treatment from a Reiki master living in my home (a story for later pages). During my time in that semi-alert state, I felt a tug on my leg that I somehow recognized as my brother, Rob. A "breeze" seemed to kick up from nowhere. I grinned to think that when he showed up he was still, as always, pulling my leg.

Julie, who was administering the treatment, said, "There's someone here."

"Yes. I know," I replied. "It's my brother, Rob."

She was quiet for a moment and then told me simply that he was not here to worry or frighten me. Rather, he wanted to make me smile, to help protect me if I would let him. I felt a rush of acceptance and gratitude, and in my heart and mind, shared with him a big hug.

Forgiveness and acceptance were the sense of the day. Ever after, when I would meet people sensitive to such things as auras, they would smile and tell me that my entourage was with me. He still is.

ROBBIE, HEY ROBBIE

chorus:
Robbie, hey Robbie,
are you leaving so soon?
Dying so suddenly
by the light of the Moon.
Hearts will be heavy,
The tears they will run,
At the loss of my brother,
My dad's only son.

verse:
Robbie and I were rambunctious kids
We did a lot of fighting, and I know
We gave Mom fits!
But he knew that she loved him
by the gifts that she gave …
From his first childhood treasures
to the flowers on his grave.

chorus repeat

I'm sure there was a second verse, but that is 41 years ago now and I never wrote the song down to save it for later. It was merely a passing expression of loss from a teenage sister.

STAGES OF MOURNING

People talk about the stages of mourning in a way that makes it sound like a series of feelings or reactions eventually leading to a kind of resolution of spirit. Or at the very least, resignation to the dull ache that carries on when the immediate crisis is over.

I remember talking to my dad in the months following Rob's death about having seen and communicated with him in the days at home after the funeral. He characterized my faith as enviable. He only wished that he could sense and believe such a thing.

Mom, on the other hand, sunk into a determined and conflicted state of grief; part guilt, part anger, part sense of being victimized. (It has taken me years to understand it.) So any expectation I might have had of being appreciated for my efforts to develop skills in useful ways in the family business were simply not acceptable to her. I suppose she was aghast at my audacity. I should have known … *that* was supposed to be the future plan for my brother. Certainly not for me.

Every time I seemed to do something well, it was a betrayal of her expertise, or expectations for Rob. She did sometimes try, with only moderate success, to hide her feelings.

As it turns out, pain is contagious. You need to find your own story.

CANYON'S EDGE

perched at canyon's edge
a bird with wounded wing
I stare unsmiling
at the colours on the rock
studying the distance and the danger

    I feel your hand
    upon my back
    not there to push
    as I might have suspected
    in the early days,
    but on its way
    to soothe and circle round me
    pull me into warmth and comfort
    perched at canyon's edge with you
            the bird lifts up
            her injuries
            to the wind

WIND SONGS

encumbered
I ascend the uphill swamp
weary from the long and arduous crawl
well-acquainted now with every
nuance of the sludge
every measure, every grudge
every sloppy, sticky
pleasure painfully taken
from my heart
in tender times

plucking out my fists
no longer smitten with the muck
I hear wind songs
my arms
extending
into sky
arching to glide
I recognize flight
can only come
with letting foothold go ...

LETTING FOOTHOLD GO

When your spirit calls you to let go and take flight, it's important to know you have the option to land somewhere. This is not to say that the heady freedom of taking flight is not an utter JOY! It is not to be missed! Choose carefully, though, where you decide to touch down for a rest from all that flapping.

Within a year of Rob's death, I got married and lived in a different town than my parents. I pulled out of university to work in a local bank to support me and my husband while he continued his education at the University of Guelph, where we'd met.

Within a few months, though, he stopped going to school and started working in a men's clothing store in town. I felt contented. We had good friends, a nice apartment, and the luxury of making our own goals and own decisions.

Rick was very interested in getting us into a starter home, humble though it might be. It seemed important to get a toehold in a real estate investment, have a chance to establish ourselves in our own home. We felt we could start our nest egg with our cars. (We each owned one.) Rick had a blue Volkswagen Beetle, and I had a Chevy Nova that my dad had bought for me after Rob's death. That may seem a weird reason to buy me a car, but let me explain.

I had gone back to school after the funeral was over. I was living off campus and used to hitch a ride to school. There was a tacit understanding among the students and professors at U of G that if one of your classmates, or a professor who recognized you, saw you with your thumb out, they'd offer a ride to school. By the same token, if you didn't recognize the driver, you simply waved them on and waited for the next opportunity.

One day that fall, Dad decided to stop by and see how I was doing on his way back from a business meeting far from home. He caught me out on the road with my thumb out. By the next weekend, he and I were at various car dealerships in Toronto, kicking tires and exploring various makes and models.

He wanted a big "Sherman Tank". I wanted something sporty. We ended up settling on a Chevy Nova. White with a red racing stripe down the side. (Pretty cool, eh?)

When he brought me the car papers to sign later that month, he told me the license plates letters read JPV. He grinned and said it stood for Junior Poopsie Vehicle.

I grinned back at him and said, "Oh, no! It stands for Just Plain Vroom!" That might help explain why, when he brought the car, he gave me a Last Will and Testament to sign. (I signed it.)

Now, back to our originally scheduled story ...

When Rick and I were thinking of coming up with the down payment for a starter home, we decided we could sell one of the cars. It certainly seemed like a good idea at the time.

The next time Dad came for a visit, we proudly showed him the little saltbox house we were ready to put an offer on. Dad's thinker got busy, and he came back with an alternative.

Dad was starting on a new project. A 54-hole golf course to be built in Stouffville, Ontario. Depending on traffic, it was 40 to 50 minutes up the road from their house. My parents, at their previous golf club, had become used to a commute of only 200 yards. They planned to move to a house beside the Stouffville golf course for efficiency's sake. I also wondered if part of this decision was because Rob had died at their current house and it was tough to be there every day.

Dad's offer to Rick and me included a job for Rick, helping him build his new course, and use of their house on Staines Road, just northeast of Toronto (a fairly large old century- -plus house.) No rent to be paid on the house ... but then again, no rights of ownership either. We simply had to move back closer to them and not try to buy the house in Guelph. Most people would say that sounds like a pretty sweet deal!

Dad did have a reputation for being able to tell a guy to go to hell and have him look forward to the trip, and this certainly didn't sound at all like hell. I felt just a twinge of regret to be climbing back into my parents' world of influence.

HOLE IN MY SOLE

A hole in the sole
Is a very bad thing.
Ask the healers and spiritual types.
It's the place where the casement
Of each of our souls
Is tied off when we're born, with a string.

If never quite finished
(perhaps born too soon)
Or kept open a little too long,
Lifelong challenges
Become our fate
And may keep us from writing our song

I want my soul NOW
I want to reclaim it
Before it cannot be done.

BLOOMING DISTRACTIONS

Rick and I spent months rearranging and adapting the house and property at Staines to suit our own style. A lot of the major things were in good shape, but we had to learn how to cope with the octopus in the basement. (Some would call it the heating system, but "octopus" seemed more apt.) The yard included a swimming pool. I had already learned to deal with the filters, pumps, etc., when Mom and Dad lived there, so that helped.

On my 21st birthday, Mom's present to me was to send me to floral design school at U of G for three weeks in the summer. I earned my Canadian Floral Design diploma and was officially qualified to work in a flower shop.

I had been in and around garden clubs, flower shows, and such with my mom since my age was in the single digits. She generously wanted to share the knowledge and training of her vocation over the previous decade or so. Instead of getting into the garden club hobby or applying for work in a florist shop, I chose to work independently.

I spent quite a few days cleaning up and preparing the old pig barn on the property for my workshop. I bought some large used fridges and was able to make use of the old mechanics counter Rob had used for working on his snowmobiles as my work bench for making floral designs. I did mostly wedding flowers for the church and receptions, and bouquets, boutonnières, and corsages for wedding parties.

Once set up, I would invite potential clients to the house to choose flowers and colours, discuss requirements, and give quotes. Wednesday mornings, I would drive out to the "Clock" (an area of wholesale floral suppliers) near Toronto's airport to pick up supplies. Once back at my shop, I'd put in as many hours as necessary (often most daylight hours), designing and assembling the flower arrangements.

Saturday was delivery day, driving to the banquet hall, the bride's house, the church, and then doing the rounds again to pick up flowers no longer needed (in the church when the party had already moved on to the reception hall).

What a joy and privilege to be working in such a medium of beauty! A few times, I worked with Mom on other floral design projects. Once we decorated a lovely old home for Christmas. I also travelled with her to Ireland to help with an international flower show. We went to New York for a similar purpose.

The joy of working with flowers was a good influence on us. That's my theory. We got along quite well on these journeys.

A CELEBRATION IN FLOWERS

In May of 2000, Mom and I travelled to the World Flower Show in Newry, considered a Catholic stronghold and located in Northern Ireland. Reverend Mac was the organizer. A Catholic seminary (Dromantine) was the location for the event, and all was under the skilled and gracious hospitality of Father Finnegan. The event was a most marvellous experience attended by a variety of nationalities and certainly deserving its own song! (Okay ... how about a parody. It's on the next page.)

I'm grateful to Mom for taking me along on this trip!

DEAR OLD DROMANTINE

Shake hands with the Reverend Mac, my dear
You'll have to stand on cue.
And Father Finnegan smiles at us,
No matter what we do!

There's plenty to see and lots to do,
and generous food and wine.
We're as welcome as the flowers in May
to dear old Dromantine.

We've been sharing hints and highly trained,
Surrounded by music and entertained.
We'll not see the likes of this again!
in dear old Dromantine.

verse 1 repeats

Sung to the tune of "Dear Old Donegal" at the closing pub night for the show. Lyrics by Cinder. Tune traditional.

JULIE JESSICA LOUISE

I hurried home to meet with you
surprised to know
that Julie is your name.
When you rode
inside my womb
and pressed insistent fingers
toes and other body parts
against my ribs,
I named you Jessica Louise,
but that's okay.
My parents didn't
give me my name either.
Not the one
I now know to be mine ...
and your father somehow
always thought
your name should have been Sarah.

I loved you and your company
when you rode round
within my womb
your stillness
signalled, so they said
a death
an ending.
Terrible loss.
But I still felt
your presence.

You were there for me to care for
and protect from those whose logic
would dictate your terms.

I hear you now,
Love.

Perhaps that's why no tombstone
marks your grave
to give you closure.
Perhaps I'm not quite up to such composure.
The final rock of recognition
might bring the admittance of the night
into a place that in my sight
is lit,
and warm,
and holds you still …

This poem was written while contemplating the loss of my daughter. She was declared "without heart-beat" in utero at about eight and a half months of development. I carried her for three weeks while we all waited to see whether my body would be triggered to reject her remains. In July of 1978, her body was delivered by C-section. The only pearl I can imagine that may have come from her death is one additional and glorious orb of light, joy, innocence, and grace … floating around Heaven all day.

WHAT NEXT?

There was no funeral service to honour our girl ... or even recognize her existence. I guess that, for Rick, it was the loss of a hope, an expectation, and other people could understand we felt sadness. For me, though, she had been much more of a living being, riding around in my womb. She danced to loud, rhythmic music (she loved concerts) and was very active, making me smile with every little kick.

While I was still in the hospital recovering from surgery, Rick came to me one day and said he had been asked about arrangements for her "disposal." He suggested we have the funeral home come and pick up her remains, and take them to be buried in common ground. I had never been allowed to see or hold her, and had to sneak a look at my chart (which was not permitted) to even know how she had died. I nodded "yes" to his suggestion. At least the hospital had not put her out with the trash.

It took me months to regain any sense of balance after her loss. In time, though, I wanted to talk about what possibilities lay ahead for me and Rick. Did we want to try for a child again? The doctors had said that, during the C-section, they'd removed a cyst from my fallopian tube, which could very well obstruct my ability to become pregnant again in the future. Rick told me that it was my body, so essentially my decision. Weeks later, we began to look into the path of adoption.

We had an interview at our home with an agent from Children's Aid to establish if we were fit to be prospective parents and had a suitable living environment for a child. The interview sparked some concerns for me about relationship issues we'd never openly discussed (much less resolved) between us. This was in early 1980, and my parents had decided they would be going down to their apartment in Florida a month later than usual that year. They offered to allow Rick and me the use of their apartment during that time.

Things felt pretty tense to me. Once down there, however, we found ourselves, one afternoon, doing the horizontal mambo (as one friend would have called it). Okay. You can guess what happened next, can't you? After a couple of weeks, I did a pregnancy test. Surprise! Baby on board! In spite of all the dire predictions—here we go again.

Life is what happens while you are making other plans.

Ironically, the adoption office contacted us during our last two weeks down south to say they might have a prospective baby for us.

Well, as a saying credited to my maternal grandfather goes: "There's a difference between scratching your ass and tearing it all to pieces." We told the agency what had happened and thanked them for their efforts, but declined.

During this pregnancy, I proceeded very carefully with my health. Every second day, I had a visit scheduled with either the OB/GYN or my diabetic specialist. Medically, things were well-monitored. On the mental/emotional level … not so much.

I became increasingly frustrated at our inability to talk about anything beyond surface practicalities. I imagine it was just as frustrating for Rick. I kept bugging him to address some of our problems, but he had no apparent idea what I wanted or needed from him. Eventually, at about six months of pregnancy, I sat down with him one day and explained that I didn't want to be losing sleep or feeling so tense. We had already lost one baby, and I wanted to protect this one from a similar fate.

We agreed to separate until the baby was safely born, and then afterwards, if we felt there was anything worth talking about, we'd talk. Not long after that, I was admitted to the hospital so a close eye could be kept on the pregnancy. At about eight months, a fetal monitor showed the baby was under stress and I agreed to meet the doctor down the hall in 15 minutes for a cesarean delivery.

The doctor asked me if there was anyone he should call. I gave him my father-in-law's number, which he wrote with a marker, right on his scrubs. A few minutes later, we were in the OR and I was being given an epidural. I wanted to be awake for the delivery, to reassure myself the baby was okay, rather than finding out later once I "came to." I was strapped to the OR table with my feet crossed and my arms spread out to the sides, with a blood pressure cuff on one arm and an IV on the other.

I had a soft-spoken Jewish doctor with a full red beard and a quiet but ever-ready sense of humour. When he came into the room, he asked, "Well ... are you ready?"

I looked at him, rolled my eyes, and said, "I gotta tell you, Doc, it's a hell-of-a way to spend Easter!" Most of the team in the room broke out laughing. Only the anesthesiologist was not happy.

"Hey!" he scolded us all. "Quiet down in here!"

I quickly shot back, "It's MY surgery! If I feel like laughing, I'm gonna do it!"

My doctor, having tested the freezing to make sure it was working, made a motion with his arm as if to saw open my belly. Then he winked at me, threw the scalpel into the corner of the room, and hollered, "Somebody bring me a SHARP one will you!"

It pleases me to think that my son entered this world in a room full of people laughing.

JASON

inside out
and upside down
a crumply heap
of fleece and cotton-poly
is left for me to contemplate
as quiet closes in

    welcome just for now
    as the echoes of the morning
    leave their sound-prints on my
    screen door slamming
    dishes rattling
    giggles rising
    to the bedroom window
    from the lawn

one small boy
rides his yellow chariot
off to school
I gather up pajamas
still warm
from last night's slumber

    I hold him safe
    within my thoughts
    as morning
    and the school bus
    move on ...

SAINT HAZEL

My Auntie Hazel would blush and wave at me to hush when I would call her that. In my childhood, and even now, she is the closest thing to a saint I'll ever know personally. Her presence in my life was a God-given blessing of the highest order. She was there, to comfort and support my mom the day I was born. She was a walking, talking, model of unconditional love for me to adore in my childhood years. She was like a second mother to my son Jason when he was just a toddler. She always welcomed him with open arms, calling him "my VERY BEST boy!"

Aunt Hazel was the head nurse in a convalescent hospital in Toronto, and the wife of my mom's brother, Bud. They were with us for most important holidays and occasions, and the subject of many happy memories for me.

One treasured memory is the day Hazel taught me the meaning and availability of forgiveness.

One weekend, when I was about seven or eight, Aunt Hazel and Uncle Bud were staying at our house with me and my brother while Mom and Dad were out at a function for the weekend.

Uncle Bud enjoyed getting a rise out of me by teasing me and watching my reaction. He really meant no harm or offense; it was just his way of having fun.

At the dinner table one night, he said to me, while looking out the window, that he could see the par 3 hole.

"I'm sorry, Uncle Bud," I said, "but you are wrong. It's par 4."

Then the two of us got into a verbal tug of war—"Is not." "Is too." "Is NOT!" "IS TOO!!"—until I was actually yelling at Uncle Bud.

This upset me, and I had no idea what to do with my emotions. So I got up from the table and headed for the door. Once outside, I felt like crying. So I headed full speed for my safe place in the forest.

As I rounded the corner of the house, I ran full speed, right into Aunt Hazel. With that, I burst into tears. She just pulled me into a hug and held on. The more I wiggled, the tighter she held me, until I finally gave in and just cried and cried. When I finally calmed down, she asked me what was wrong.

I explained in a sobbing voice that I had yelled at Uncle Bud ... and I knew that was wrong ... and I was really sorry ... but I didn't know what to do!

She looked at me, her face reassuring and calm, and said, "Why don't you go back and just tell him you are sorry? It'll be okay."

I looked at my aunt with stunned disbelief but went to do as I was told. No one was left in the dining room. With some trepidation, I searched around the house and finally found Uncle Bud in the recreation room in the easy chair, reading his newspaper.

I stood quietly beside the ottoman, shifting from foot to foot, not wanting to interrupt his reading. When he realized I was there, he slowly folded his paper in his lap.

"What's up, Kiddo?" he asked, with a curious but calm look on his face.

I tried to explain. "I'm sorry that I yelled at you … I really didn't MEAN to, and I am so, so, SO sorry!" I was sobbing as I tried to say the words.

He waited to see if more was coming, then he reached out his big hand and ruffled my hair, saying, "Oh, I could never stay mad at you, Kiddo. It's all okay."

In a very small voice, I said, "Thank you, Uncle Bud," and wandered back out to the patio, contemplating what had happened. I had misbehaved. Then Aunt Hazel had HUGGED me! Then, I told Uncle Bud I was sorry, and he listened! AND THEN HE FORGAVE ME! I'd never been forgiven before. It felt amazing! I must have slept exceedingly well that night.

Years later, at the wedding reception for me and Rick, Hazel saved the day yet again. There were 105 people from Rick's family at the wedding, and ten of our young friends. I had less than ten family members to my name. At the end of the evening, all the guests formed a big circle at one end of the room. Rick and I stood in the middle of the circle, wearing our going-away outfits, and various guests came up to wish us well. Rick stood as his aunts and cousins ran over to him one by one, gave him a big hug and kiss, and said good-bye. I stood beside and slightly behind him … and watched.

Suddenly a very distinctive, high-pitched voice cut through the air. "I'LL KISS YOU, HONEY!"

Aunt Hazel, looking and sounding for all the world like Edith Bunker from the TV sitcom *All in the Family*, came a-running with her arms outstretched and a big smile on her face.

Thus, I was appropriately blessed by the VERY BEST hugger in the place.

OUT OF THE MOUTHS

In 1984, I was working as a real estate agent in Thornhill, Ontario. Truth be known, I was probably not really cut out for it. I loved finding a new home for people or helping them sell one; I just wasn't good enough when it was important to be tough and watch your own back.

In any case, while I gave that job a try, Aunt Hazel took care of wee Jason (as she referred to him) at her home. He called us both Ma, and only a subtle change in intonation differentiated our identities.

One fine afternoon in April, I took Jason to his Mini-Skool half-day nursery school not far from my office. We gave Aunt Hazel a ride to a nearby mall, where she planned to go shopping for a new navy slip to wear with her darker-coloured dresses. She was cheery and looking forward to her shopping. After dropping the two of them off, I went to work for several hours, and then stopped home briefly before going back to pick up Jason.

When I got home, my dad was waiting for me on my front step. That was unusual and made me wonder what was going on. I invited him into the kitchen. He looked at me with a sombre face and told me he had some bad news. Hazel had passed on.

My heart crumpled.

Evidently, Hazel had gone home when she finished her shopping.

She did find the slip she wanted ... it was beside her on the bed.

When Bud came home that afternoon, he had found her there, on her bed, looking like she had just laid down for a nap. When he couldn't wake her, he realized she was gone. Nobody thought I should be told over the phone, so Dad came to break the news.

Once I could breathe properly, I called Bud, who asked me if I'd come over to help him plan what he should do next. He told me, "Bring Jason if you need to. He shouldn't feel left out. It will be hard enough for him."

I went over to the Mini-Skool to pick up my son. I asked the lady in charge if we could use her office for a few minutes since I had to have a very difficult conversation with my son. She readily agreed, and, next thing I knew, I was sitting there, trying to figure out how to tell my three and a half year old such a thing. He stood by my knees, watching my eyes well up with tears as I told him that Auntie Hazel's heart had stopped while she was asleep, that she had died and her heart couldn't be fixed.

He looked at me with an expression of deep understanding and said, "So she's gone to Heaven to live in God's house, right?"

Hazel was a devout Catholic, and so I said, "Yes, Honey. That's probably exactly what Auntie Hazel would say." He then raised his hand to gently wipe the tears from my face.

"Don't cry, Mommy," he said. "She visits God's house all the time. Sometimes I get to go with her. He'll look after her ... she'll be okay."

Oh, my. Out of the mouth of a babe.

72 HOURS

Rick sat on a stool at the door of our son's room in the ICU. I leaned on the wall beside him, listening with rapt attention for whatever words of encouragement or information the doctor might give us. His voice came across what seemed a great expanse of space.

"This disease, and particularly the form of the disease which your son is manifesting, has a very high mortality rate. It is highly unlikely that we will see a recovery on his part. Do you understand what I am saying?"

I looked into the eyes of Dr. Cox. They were kind but firm, with a gentle detachment that comes, I suppose, from having to deliver this message on a regular basis. Internally, I reeled under the impact of not only his words, but also the incredible speed and surreal churning of events over the last couple of days.

Two nights before, I had been resting in bed, settling down for the evening, when the phone rang. It was the nurse from Jason's school. He had been brought back early from a camping trip with a number of boys from his school. She said he was feeling poorly, a little feverish and achy, and probably had the flu, as had some of his fellow students.

I speculated that his symptoms were probably enhanced by anxiety he'd felt about the week's events and perhaps exhaustion from late nights spent participating in a school play the previous weekend.

The nurse explained she was going home and didn't think he should be left alone in the infirmary. She understood that, because of my limited night vision, I didn't feel comfortable driving the highway at night and kindly offered to take him home with her if I couldn't get there to pick him up. I chose instead to call my parents, who lived closer to the school and asked them to go get him.

I thought my mom and dad could take care of Jason through the night with some TLC, plenty of fluids, and something to reduce the fever, and I would pick him up first thing in the morning. I was not overly concerned, him being in good hands and flu, colds, and such being normal and manageable.

Still, a little, nagging tingle of anxiety haunted me as I told my husband about the call when he got home. I went to bed with the thought that I would feel better when I could get my son home in the morning. I could not have been more wrong.

In the middle of the night, the phone rang again. This time, it was my dad. He had given Jason some Tylenol and put him to bed several hours earlier, but the fever was not coming down and he wanted to know what I wanted him to do. A cool bath to get his body temperature down was my advice, though, I suspected Jason would not enjoy it much, being thirteen years old and probably considering himself beyond the age for such ministrations. Nevertheless, it's what I suggested, and Dad went off to do it.

Before long, he was calling again to report he couldn't get Jason to the bath. This seemed odd. He further explained that Jason couldn't tolerate being moved. In fact, he cried out in pain when Dad would even sit on the edge of the bed. I asked him to check if he had a rash or looked swollen anywhere, and he reported that Jason's legs looked bruised. Dad wondered if he'd been beaten up at school.

This combination of symptoms, bruises, and crying out, which was not Jason's style at all, was quite beyond my ability to diagnose or contend with. I asked whether Dad knew a doctor well enough to call him at this late hour, and he suggested he'd call our old family doctor, since they were also good friends. The next phone call I received from Dad was to tell me that he and Mom were taking Jason to the hospital on the doctor's advice.

By then, it was early morning and almost time for dawn to break. I threw on some clothes, got my purse and a few essentials, and headed down the road to meet them at the hospital. It took a little over two hours to drive to the hospital and, on my way, I called the hospital several times to see if I could learn anything about what was going on.

After several calls left me with no details and only vague assurances that he was in good hands, real fear set in that this was no ordinary sickness. Dread hovered over me like a blanket of fog.

On his last phone call, my dad said they might be taking Jason to the Hospital for Sick Children in Toronto, but not likely until after I'd arrived. I phoned Rick, Jason's father, to whom I was no longer married but who still shared the raising of our son. I asked him to stay where I could reach him by phone rather than go out of the city to Jason's hospital, since it seemed likely that Jason would end up downtown. Rick would be closer to Sick Kids' from his home.

When I finally arrived at the hospital near my parent's place, I abandoned the car in the parking lot and ran to Emergency. Dad was waiting outside for me.

He walked toward me, took my hand in his, and said, "Slow down. There's not much you can do for him in a hurry. Did you get the car parked okay?"

As he walked me into the hospital, I felt a cold blast go through me. I might be losing my son. Perhaps he was already gone.

Dad pointed me toward Jason's room. I saw my mom with a mask over her mouth, standing at the side of a gurney, and heard her say, "Here she is, Honey," as she moved out of the way to let me in beside my child.

Jason was lying on his side, his eyes half-open. His face was covered with pox and perfectly still, except for his lips as he said in a tiny voice, "Hi, Mom. I really hurt. What's happening, Mom?"

His pain was palpable in the room, and I did not dare touch his body for fear of hurting him more. I laid my hand, feather-light, upon his hair and said, "I don't know what's happening yet, Hon, but I will find out and then I'll be right back, okay?" He tried to nod but winced with pain so just murmured his assent as I left to find the doctor in charge.

The doctor had apparently been informed of my arrival because we met at the doorway to the emergency room. He brought me up to date on what had been discovered and planned so far. The doctor, a pediatric specialist who'd been at the hospital when Jason arrived, told me my son was a very sick young man.

Dr. Panzer had been in the operating room when Jason was brought in and, upon hearing Jason's symptoms, rushed to the emergency room to see for himself. Dr. Panzer explained to me that he had done his graduate thesis for his pediatric specialty on meningitis. In his opinion, that's what Jason was suffering with now.

I had heard of spinal meningitis but didn't have much knowledge of the disease or its various forms. Dr. Panzer told me it could be bacterial or viral, that apparently there were many forms of the disease. A spinal tap would be taken to establish with certainty what form of the disease we were dealing with. In the meantime, the doctor was quite sure his diagnosis was correct and a delay to wait for confirmation could be fatal, so he had already started an IV and begun administering fluids, the first step in treatment.

He told me that a team of doctors and nurses would be arriving soon by helicopter from the Hospital for Sick Children. They would be establishing a breathing tube for an artificial lung and administering a drug to render Jason paralyzed and put him into a state where they could proceed with the intensive drug therapy required to try to save him.

I went back to my son. He looked at me through half-closed eyes and said, "This hurts so bad. Can't they just put me to sleep? Why is this happening?"

I told him the doctors knew that he was hurting and would soon be able to put him to sleep, but they had to wait for a team coming from Sick Kids' Hospital. I told him they would get here as quickly as they could in a helicopter, and then they would then take him with them back to Sick Kids'.

Again he said, "Why is this happening?"

I told him that his body had quite a war going on inside it. I gave him a mental picture, describing a germ multiplying into a whole army of germs, and how his body was mounting a battle against these germs with antibodies and every other ammunition it could muster, and that the pain was unfortunate but inevitable, considering the terrible battle going on inside him.

"But Mom." He sounded exhausted and weak, as if he were trying to be patient with my apparent misunderstanding of his question. "Why is this happening to me?"

Tears welled up in my eyes as I looked at him lying there. Oh, what faith our children have in us, to think we have the answers to such questions. I looked away for a moment, groping for an answer, knowing there really wasn't one but also knowing just how desperately he needed to hear it.

Finally, I looked back at my thirteen-year-old son and said, "Sweetie, shit happens. I am so very sorry that this time it is happening to you. You haven't done anything to deserve it. Sometimes bad stuff just happens. I don't know why. If I did, I would tell you."

He grew quiet and closed his eyes for a while. I stood there beside him, my hand hovering over his head, and told him that I loved him. The wait for the team from Sick Kids' seem to last forever for both of us. Every minute or two he would open his eyes and ask, "Are they here yet? How much longer?"

Suddenly the team was there. His gurney was surrounded by people arranging machines, talking numbers, keeping a patter of reassuring words flowing toward my son. I stepped out of the room while they established the airway and prepared him for the flight.

My parents were in the hall by the emergency desk. I could only imagine the horror of this event for them. I was impressed with their strength under the circumstances, but not surprised. Their strength had been tested before, and they always came through somehow. They seem to have passed some of that strength on to me. At that moment, I fervently hoped that Jason had picked up more than his share of strength from the gene pool. It was blatantly apparent he was going to need it.

The transport team came out of the ER with Jason on a gurney. One of the team explained there was not room for me to travel with them in the helicopter, so I should say good-bye to Jason for now and meet them downtown. Jason was already immobilized, tubes in place, in an altered state of consciousness.

Just in case he could hear me, or perhaps just because I needed to say something, I said, "Fly well, Sweetie. I'll see you downtown." Without saying it aloud, I added a prayer from my heart. "Please be alive when we get there."

Dr. Panzer told me it would take some time for them to get Jason set up in ICU at the hospital, so not to set any speed records driving downtown since I would probably have to wait to see him.

I wanted to get going right away. Dad insisted on driving me downtown and suggested taking my car. My mom would take their car home, get changed, and then come down to pick him up later. I wanted to just get going and drive. The urge to DO something rather than be passive was strong. However, he was probably right, and I handed over my keys.

I called Rick from the car. By now, he was very anxious for more information, and I told him as much as we knew so far. He said he would go straight to the Hospital for Sick Children to be there when they arrived with Jason. I agreed to meet him at ICU as soon as we could get there.

I called my husband, Allan, to tell him what was happening. He agreed to stay near the phone so that, once I knew what was happening at the hospital, I could call again and tell him if there was anything I needed from home. He could bring it when he came down.

We were being so organized and logical about all of this on one level, while on another level, the Earth was spinning slightly off centre.

As I found my way to the ICU from the front entrance, I turned my thoughts for a moment to Rick. We had lost a baby girl, stillborn, two years before Jason's birth. The pain of possibly losing this child as well was just too much to contemplate.

As I turned the corner into the ICU parent lounge, I saw Rick sitting there, waiting. He stood up. I went to him and we hugged, hard.

"We've been here once already," I said. "It just CAN'T happen again. Surely God wouldn't let it happen again."

We sat down together to wait, repeatedly checking with the volunteer at the desk about when we could go be with our son. She patiently reassured us she would let us know when it was okay to see him. Finally, she told us we could proceed. A nurse came and led us to Jason's ICU room. She stopped us in the hall outside to give us instructions on how to gown up, wash our hands, and don masks before entering the room.

The sound of muted machinery emanated from Jason's room, along with little beeps and whooshes. I tried to prepare myself for the sight that would greet us. Seeing him lying inert on the bed, with tubes and tape and machines on, and in and around him, my mind flashed back to his first days on this Earth.

He had been born prematurely, and his first baby pictures show his tiny face taped and tubed with IV tubes and sensors invading his body. Tubes or no tubes, he had been a wonder to me then, and now, here he was, once again hooked up to this bizarre array of machinery. He was much bigger now, just at the threshold of his teen years, but still my child, and still a wonder to me.

He was so quiet, not moving or making a sound of his own. It was as though he was in a state of suspended animation, while the machines around him kept up the steady pattern of noise—the artificial lung labouring as it filled and emptied his lungs for him, the heart monitor beeping rhythmically. The other monitor screens, which the nurse explained were measuring his blood pressure, blood density, and nerve function, among other things, displayed their graphs and numbers, adding an occasional *ping* to the chorus of life support around him.

The nurse did her best to familiarize us with the various machines and explained that, although Jason could not respond with any movement or voice, it was likely he could hear us speak and that, even though he might not remember what was said, it would be a good idea to be as positive and comforting as possible.

After that initial introduction, Rick and I fell into a pattern of taking turns being in the room with Jason while the other took care of things like making phone calls, to family, to Jason's school, to Rick's work, etc.

Jason's school had to undergo an extensive program, with the help of government health authorities, to track down any students or staff members who might have been in contact with Jason over the previous few days. A powerful drug would be administered to prevent anyone else from getting meningitis. Some of the students were travelling on school trips to England, among other places, and the process was a challenging one. Our family members also took this drug. Fortunately, these efforts were successful, and as far as we know, no one fell victim to the disease as a result of contact with Jason.

By late afternoon on that first day, my husband, Allan, arrived and was given the initial briefing about the routine in Jason's room. Other family members were in the parent lounge outside ICU to lend whatever moral support they could.

The hours blurred. Night and day became irrelevant in the rhythm of being with Jason, talking to him, singing to him, gently stroking his hand and legs. I did my best to remember what I had learned about healing touch in a course I'd taken years earlier and spent hours doing whatever I knew or could think of to try to direct healing energy toward Jason, to assist him in the terrible battle he was fighting.

Several people visited in that first 24 hours. Karen Bach, a minister and family friend, used her theologian privileges to get into the ICU. She stood and prayed for a time at the end of Jason's bed while I continued to do healing touch techniques. She didn't say much, just stood there and prayed, and then quietly left the room, but her presence was supportive and a comfort.

I was in the room with Jason when Allan came in to tell me that a young man dressed in the blazer and flannels of Jason's school had shown up in the parent lounge. It was the captain of the #1 hockey team at Jason's school. Jason was an enthusiastic fan and would have been thrilled to think that this young lad cared enough about him to show up at the hospital bearing a hockey stick signed by all the members of the #1 team. He was there to give it to Jason as a symbol of their affection and support.

Although we couldn't let him into Jason's room, we did take the hockey stick in, placed it in the corner of the room, and told Jason about it, just in case he could hear us. A staff member at the school also called to tell us that the boys of the school, had, on their own initiative and without any direction from the staff, been holding a vigil for Jason in the school's chapel. The boys had taken turns maintaining this vigil around the clock, keeping a candle lit for him. Apparently they were determined to keep this going until they heard good news of a recovery.

As the hours wore on, we realized that, to keep our strength up, we had to take turns getting some rest. Being a diabetic, I had to take some time out to do the various tests, injections, food intake, etc., required to keep me going. In the parent lounge, the sofas became little camps for the various families who, like us, were trying to cope with a very sick child in the ICU.

That lounge was a community unto itself. Total strangers only hours before, we were now all bound in a common struggle—a nightmare punctuated with bits of news about one child or another, the devastation of a turn for the worse, the spark of hope in some small improvement in a daughter's or son's condition.

There was an atmosphere of enormous compassion, mutual support, and quiet courage. We were all determined that, somehow, by sheer will and love, we could help our children survive. We cried together, hugged together, shared supplies, blankets, and stories, and just shared this rarefied space, with an intense respect for the crisis we all were enduring.

There were parents whose children did not make it. All of us felt the emptiness those parents held in their souls as they left the lounge with their belongings and tried to go out to face the day with their grief.

There was a woman whose baby had miraculously survived a terrible medical ordeal and was being transferred to a regular room in the hospital. That woman, whose name I didn't know, came over to me as she was leaving the ICU area and gave me a lapel pin. It was a little golden angel. She simply said that she hoped and prayed this little guardian angel would be with and take care of my son as it had her own child, and that we would be okay. I wore that guardian angel close to my heart for the duration of our time in the ICU.

Meanwhile, Jason remained in his state of paralysis, the doctors coming from time to time to make adjustments in the doses of medication flowing into his veins.

We gradually learned more about his disease. It was explained to us that Jason had a bacterial form of the disease called "meningococcal septicemia." The disease caused a cascade of symptoms in the body, which included a dangerously high heart rate, loss of circulation to the body (particularly the extremities), and damage to the entire vascular system, which compromised the body's ability to get oxygen and other nutrients to tissues and organs, and possibly to the brain and nervous system. This could result in the failure or death of any or all of the affected areas.

Jason's blood pressure at one point was at 83/80, which is almost a complete shutdown, and his heart rate was extremely high. This was during the second day in the ICU, and it was at this time that Dr. Cox took me and Rick out into the hall to tell us that we should prepare ourselves for Jason's death.

The doctor said there was a team of cardiac and other surgeons considering an experimental procedure that, with our permission, they would like to try with

Jason since, at that point, there seemed little else anyone could do that had not already been done.

I asked Dr. Cox how long, in his opinion, Jason could live in his present condition. After a thoughtful pause, he said that, although there were never specific, accurate answers to such questions, he thought it could be as much as a few hours or as little as 20 minutes.

It took a moment to absorb that answer. Rick was understandably silenced by it.

I found myself telling Dr. Cox I wanted him to get the crowd of people out of Jason's room and that, with the exception of the one nurse required to watch the monitors, we wanted five minutes alone with our son.

"Give us five minutes," I said, "and if nothing has changed in that five minutes, then you bring on the cardiac surgeons or do anything else you can think of that might help, be it experimental or whatever. But first, please, let us spend that five minutes alone with our son."

Dr. Cox, looked into my eyes for a moment, then, without saying a word, nodded, went quietly into the room, and ushered out the team of doctors, technicians, and other staff. They walked away down the hall.

Rick and I looked at each other and turned to enter Jason's room. I noticed Rick's knees seemed to have gone weak, and I said to him, in a voice which sounded infinitely stronger than I would have expected, "NO! You stand up!" and then a little more softly but with a sense of assurance that came from some unknown source, "You stand up, and you fill your mind with a picture of his heart, beating, strong, and rhythmic, and don't you let go of that thought. You keep it beating in your head. Can you do that?" Rick nodded, and we went over to the bed and stood beside Jason as he lay inert and fragile.

All sense of time and awareness of our physical surroundings disappeared as we stood there. I felt Rick standing tall behind me, and I turned my focus to channel as much positive energy as I could tap into, through my heart and mind, and spirit, into that young son of ours in front of me. In my mind, I sent messages to the people who had loved him and passed on, like his Aunt Hazel and his Grandpa Bud, telling them, "We are not through with him here on Earth yet. Please, do what you can to send him back to us."

I prayed to whatever forces in the universe govern such things to give him life, give him a chance to have more time here on this Earth to grow and learn, and laugh. I tried to bring into the room the love and prayers, and all the positive thoughts being held out to him by family and friends, both nearby and faraway, who had expressed their love and support for him.

As the intensity of this effort grew, the room seemed to buzz with energy. It was something I can only describe as a brilliance lighting the air as if with a strobe light. I don't know exactly how long we were held in that light, in that intensity, but I was startled back to physical awareness by the sound of buzzers and bells. In the next breath, the room was crowded again, as doctors and staff rushed in around Jason's bed and began adjusting chemicals and machinery.

They talked softly but urgently to each other as they performed their complicated tasks. Rick and I quietly moved back to the corner of the room and stood watching. We were both stunned, I think, by the speed with which events were unfolding. We couldn't be sure whether all of this activity indicated a turn for the better, or for the worse. For the next few minutes, we hovered in the doorway or just outside in the hall.

One of the nurses, who had been in Jason's room with us, said to us as she went by that things had really started to move and they might be busy in there for a while. Finally, after what was no doubt less than an hour but seemed like forever, Dr. Cox came out and told us the team of doctors had decided there was perhaps some reason to hope after all. He said that, if Jason could get beyond the mark of 72 hours after his initial onset, there might be good reason to be optimistic.

I felt a combination of exhaustion and hope wash through me as we settled ourselves to continue this journey. We had just over 24 hours to go to make it past the stipulated 72-hour mark. The question of "then what?" had not yet entered my mind.

Dr. Nakagawa, a brilliant intensivist who I came to think of as The Juggler, continued to adjust the various medications as they flowed in and out of our son. We let our friends and families know that there was still hope but no guarantees, and continued to take turns being with Jason and taking short cat naps in the parent lounge, or at least resting when sleep was impossible.

From time to time, the doctors performed various tests, some which must have been extremely painful for Jason. We were unsure of how much the medications would dull his perception or memory of the pain. It was awful to consider the horror of causing more suffering for this very sick boy of ours.

At one point, while we waited outside in the hall during a seemingly endless test, we heard some very wise and comforting words from a visiting Israeli doctor who stopped to talk to Rick.

"So," he said, "you have a son in pain. This is very difficult. The good news is that you have a son, in pain." He left us to consider the implications of that remark.

Later on, as the 72-hour mark approached, this same Dr. Ali, whose full name I never did learn, talked to us about his experiences with meningitis in the Middle East, where the outbreak of the disease is a yearly occurrence. Based on his extensive experience, he told us, in a tone which was at the same time encouraging and mischievously conspiratorial, "This guy," pointing in the direction of Jason's bed, "this one is over the hump." He then winked at us, smiled, and walked away. This man was not officially Jason's doctor, but he had been watching his case with interest, and we clung to those positive words with such hope and faith that it helped us keep our spirits up through the remaining wait for the official word.

Finally, as the hour we had waited for passed, Dr. Cox met us in the hallway outside Jason's room. He looked at us and calmly said, "It would appear that Jason is likely to survive this initial stage of the disease. There will be further treatments to be done. We won't know the full extent of damage until the diseased areas have become further delineated, but we can discuss that as things go along."

Rick and I stood there, mute, waiting, since it was evident that he had more to say. After a long pause, in which he looked into our eyes intently, he asked, "Did you understand what I was saying to you here yesterday?"

I responded, "Yes. You were trying to tell us that he was dying."

The doctor nodded.

"However," I said, "I am not ready to let go of the other end of that rope."

Dr. Cox, with a gentle smile of understanding, said, "Yes. So I noticed."

He slowly walked away down the hall, nodding his head. After several weeks in intensive care, while the disease delineated the areas of damage to be contended with, Jason was finally able to be moved to a hospital room on 8C, where plastic surgery patients and other children requiring reconstructive work were cared for.

Before taking our leave of the parents' lounge in the ICU, I passed on the guardian angel pin to a mother from overseas. She and her family had lived not far from the area where the Chernobyl nuclear disaster had taken place and now her daughter was suffering from what they suspected were the after-effects of the radiation she'd been exposed to.

Although the mother spoke no English and I speak no Russian, she understood very clearly the meaning of the angel pin. We held each other's gaze in mutual understanding and compassion for a long moment before I got up to follow Jason to his new location.

The months that followed were filled with pain, anxiety, moments of hope, and nights of despair. The staff at the Hospital for Sick Children, our families, and friends did all they could to assist us. Jason and all of our hearts and minds somehow made their way through the terrible treatments, necessary surgeries, and difficult therapy sessions.

In the final analysis, our son spent almost six months at the hospital as an in-patient, and many more in continued recovery at home. He was left with a large portion of his body's surface scarred and skin-grafted. The fingers of his right hand are gone, all but the thumb and a short stub remaining of the index finger. His right foot still requires special padding to allow him to walk, since the tissue that would normally pad his heel is gone, as is the smallest toe and the bones of the foot that would normally connect to it. Many stories remain to be told of the journey that followed.

The truth of it still has a powerful impact on me whenever I think of or spend time with my son. I am filled with wonder and gratitude that he is still with us, here, on this Earth. So many bits of synchronic-ity—the influence of the right people ministering to him at the right time, the wonders of modern medi-cine, and the energy, love, and hope of all of us who love that young man, worked in harmony to provide us all with proof positive that miracles do happen.

I am pleased to know such a miracle personally. He is my son.

Jason Macmillan Hammond, in 1994, presented with
the prestigious Tilston Award for courage
and tenacity
during the commencement exercises at his school
following his ordeal:
St. Andrew's College, Aurora.
"Acquit Ye like Men"
(school motto)

BEWARE THE UNDER TOAD

Beyond the business and busy-ness of trying to achieve some sense of re-integration into normalcy in our lives, this experience took us through some extraordinary events. Is there a road back? Or do you gather up the pieces of what has been saved along with what has been learned and try to move forward from there?

I had spent months with the bulk of my attention and focus on my son and his progress. Other parts of my life had been neglected, and I was left with a couple of unsettled issues to consider.

My marriage, for one, had suffered damage. Allan and I had been married less than two years when Jason became ill. My husband experienced a serious deficit in the amount of time and attention that he'd grown to expect from me as a newlywed. It was no doubt a harsh change. He showed great compassion for Jason's situation, but it certainly turned the newly established routine of our blended family on its head.

Allan underwent real soul searching, asking himself such questions as "Are you doing what you really want to do with your own life?" We'd had a reminder that life itself can be all too fragile. Allan came to feel that he was not really happy being a lawyer, but he wasn't sure what to tackle instead. My dad heard him speak of that. The offer that followed was eerily familiar. Dad offered Allan a chance to give up his current practice as a lawyer and just cut the rough on a tractor at the new golf project for the upcoming summer.

Allan had responsibilities to pay child support and alimony from his previous marriage. I offered to support the two of us, even if we had to live in a cold-water flat, while he took two years to either educate or train for whatever work he chose as his new direction. Dad offered him enough pay to at least cover his support payments, and Allan chose to take him up on his offer.

My "Spidey Sense" was sounding alarms. However, he looked happy to just drive a tractor for the summer, and I was exhausted from the adventures we'd gone through with my son. Allan began working for Dad not long after. In the meantime, a couple of things happened that would alter my life's course quite profoundly.

COMING HOME

The medical team at the Hospital for Sick Children had informed me Jason could likely come home within the next couple of weeks. I took a midweek trip for a couple of days to my home in Muskoka to organize some things in the house that Jason would need.

As I drove out of the city, I took a detour so I could drive past St. James Cemetery in Toronto. I had done some research and found out that the remains of my daughter, Julie Jessica Louise, had been buried in "common ground" in that cemetery in 1978. That was 16 years ago, and I had never gone looking for her burial site before. Something in the months spent so close to losing my son had made me want to find closure with my daughter.

I pulled into St. James, parked the car, and walked around for a while, wondering where was the area considered common ground. I didn't even know whether her remains had been put in a container, or cremated, or just buried in the state they were in when picked up from the hospital.

After wandering a bit, I saw a gardener working quietly on some gardens near a gravesite. We exchanged nods, and I asked him if he worked for the cemetery and knew where the common ground was. I also asked if the grave he was making so beautiful was related to him personally somehow.

He straightened up, stretched, leaned on his garden tool, and settled his shoulders. "Well, there's more than one such area in here." He gazed around, and pointed over toward a stand of trees. "That's one area, right over there. There's a half dozen or so. Why do you ask?" I ended up telling him about my daughter, the abridged version, anyway.

He looked pensive for a moment and said, "We might be able to find out where she is, if you want to try." I looked at him, wide-eyed, and just nodded silently. "Okay then, off we go."

The man led me over to a little brick building not far away, and we went inside. Under an old counter, where a number of books were stored on large shelves, he pulled out an old ledger.

"Give me the names again," he said. "Her father's, too ... and yours at the time." His old, weathered hand ran down the page until he arrived at the right date. Sure enough, he found her record of interment.

"Shall we go then?" I nodded again and followed him out into the vast sea of gravestones. "There won't be a gravestone, of course," he said, "but most of these sites have a little marker at their corner. Your child's will have the number 33 on it." He led me on quite a long walk at an unhurried pace until we found number 33.

The gardener said gently, "Well, I'll leave you to 'er now."

I murmured a "thank you" and stood there, staring at the ground.

I stood at the spot where my daughter's remains had been returned to the Earth. I looked up. We were at the edge of a small stand of trees. Tall enough to have been there when she arrived. They were deciduous trees. Beech, I thought, and their leaves from last fall were still lying on the ground, covering much of the grass. I was glad she was near trees.

I began gathering damp leaves from around her spot and cleared a small area near the marker with my fingers. As I was doing this, I apologized to her for taking so long to get there.

One by one, in the clear spot created, I placed a yellowed leaf. With each one I remembered one experience from the days when I carried her. Her dancing in my belly at the concert. The day we flew the kite her Aunt Gaye had made in the yard at Staines Road. The pretty pink dress I wore when her dad and I went to Disney World with her in my belly. There were lots of moments that came to mind.

I formed these storied leaves into the shape of a heart and meditated for a while near them. Then I stood up and sang her an Irish Lullaby. "Toorah loorah loorah." I slowly walked back to my car, looked for the gardener to blow him a thank-you kiss, and got into the car.

After taking a few minutes to be sure I was calm and alert and ready to drive, I continued on my way back along the cemetery road. As I was driving along, approaching the street but not yet at the entrance, I found myself quietly talking, as if to my daughter.

I called her Jessica Louise, which was the name I'd hoped to give her if she had been born healthy. My heart skipped a beat when a clear teenage girl's voice sounded behind me.

"It's Julie, if you don't mind!"

It was spoken in the gently scornful tone only a teenage girl with one hand on hip and toe tapping can produce. I stopped the car and sat there, mouth agape. Finally mustering my voice, I asked, "Can I still use Jessica Louise as kind of middle names?"

"Yeah, sure."

I didn't look behind me. I knew I wouldn't see her. But I also knew she was there, as surely as I knew I was there with her. She did not speak again for the rest of the ride home, but my thoughts filled with words that I needed to keep. I got off the highway and stopped at a rest stop, writing down the words so I wouldn't lose them before I got home. They can be found in my poem, "Julie Jessica Louise."

I was then able to settle down enough to complete the drive home, where I set about taking in my suitcase and one of the Beech leaves to preserve.

When the phone rang, it was my friend Ken calling. He warned me to hear him out, since he guessed that my first impulse might be to say "no" to his suggestion.

"Okay, Ken-man," I chuckled, "so, what's your suggestion?"

He told me about a young woman from our town who, some time ago, had moved out to the West Coast of Canada. She was going to be in town for a while to resolve some things with her family but didn't want to be living in their house while doing it. She had gone to Ken to see if he knew of a place near the water that might be available to rent. Maybe an unoccupied cottage somewhere on a lake.

Ken was on a mission. "You have that big house right on the river," he said, "and I just wondered if maybe you'd be willing to rent her a room or something."

"Oh, Kenny," I sighed heavily, "you KNOW I have always avoided that. We're getting close to being able to bring Jason home … and I really just want to get back to normal."

Ken waited patiently on the other end of the phone line while I talked myself in and out of the idea several times. (We knew each other pretty well!) Eventually, I sighed again and said, "I don't know Ken. If you want, tell her to come over this afternoon and we'll have a cup of tea … and I'll think about it. No promises, though! I have a lot to sort out."

After we hung up, I sat at the big window, looking out at the river and let my mind float freely. I began to think about the other question that had followed me over that last few months.

Was the experience in the ICU with Jason exclusive to that situation? The appearance of healing light in the room, the response of his bodily symptoms to the energy I was trying to focus and deliver to him from the Heavens, from other peoples' prayers and vigils … Did he respond so undeniably because it was coming from his mom? Or was there an opportunity to be able to heal not only my own son, but others as well? What would I call that? How would I offer it? What if it was a one-time gift in my life?

All of this was rolling around in my thoughts when my reverie was interrupted by a knock on the door. I went and opened it, and saw a lovely young woman standing on the front step. Her face brightened.

She smiled at me and said, "Hi! I'm Julie!"

I stood there with the hair on the back of my neck bristling. Before either of us said another word, we found ourselves hugging as if we were two long-lost beloveds and weeping there in the doorway.

After a bit of time, we released each other just a little, to look at each other's face. I realized we hadn't left the threshold of the door yet and said, "I guess you better come in!" We both laughed and went into the kitchen for tea. Julie ended up living there at my house for the better part of three years.

So many synchronicities and connections between us were to be discovered. One of those was that she had an answer to my thoughts and wonderings about the energy healing experience with Jason. It turns out Julie is a Reiki Master.

Over the next years, Jules lived in my home on the river. I provided accommodation, and we provided each other with much-needed, deep kinship. She also schooled me in the practices and understanding of Reiki.

By the time she left to go back to Salt Spring Island on the West Coast, I had reached the third-level atunement in Reiki myself. By that time my marriage had ended and Allan had moved out. What had been the girls' bedroom became the Reiki Room, where I provided Reiki to various clients in the community. It remained as such until it was time to leave that home years later.

HEALER, TEACHER

Healer, teacher
leader, friend
you laugh with me
and have no fear it seems
to hold my hand.
We journey through
this heart of mine
explorers in a place
where I have put
and you may find
convolutions
which have taken
me through storms
and other danger zones
too hideous
to mention at the time.
Wisdom
sitting close at hand
with readiness to listen
makes it possible
for you to see the
nature of the beast.
Resolution,
I may find here
comfort
and, perhaps,
release

MUSKOKA TIME

Over the next several years, we lived in a house on the river that seemed to take on its own persona. People who visited were heard to say they could feel themselves take a deep breath and relax just by coming into the great room with its huge windows overlooking the water.

In the summers, I would often hang out in the screened-in room off the kitchen. From there, you could see the river and the oxbow lake forming on the river's elbow to the north of the house. You could also hear the sounds that surrounded the place, whether it was the calls of loons on a quiet weekday evening or the squeals of the summer people roaring down the river in their boats on their way to enjoy Lake Muskoka.

The place did hold a wonderful energy. Alive, and yet tranquil. I got even more involved in local theatre, musicals and dinner theatre, directing and some-times acting in a variety of roles. Give me a nice, juicy character role or a comical bit and I am a happy girl!

I also played golf again. I was a member of a local semi-private club and, for a couple of terms, served on their board of directors. I even won the Ladies' Club Championship one summer! It had been a while since I'd had a win like that. Over time, four of us in the Ladies' section became a fearsome four-some, playing together regularly. It was during this rather idyllic interlude in Muskoka that I first became aware of Dr. Jean Houston.

I saw her one day on a wild feed pick-up on my satellite TV from a channel in California called the Wisdom Channel. Her intelligence, humour, wisdom, and depth of understanding in a very broad range of topics just knocked me out. I was so impressed that I was still talking about her one afternoon when I went into town for an appointment with a friend who was a life coach.

As I went on about Dr. Houston, she gave me a look that said she was way ahead of me.

"Oh, yes! Jean!" she said. "Yes, I think she's at Omega this weekend."

"What's Omega?" I asked.

She described the beautiful rustic grounds of a campus for adult learning that brought in presenters for meditation, dance, music, creativity, and a whole range of workshops. She then fetched her copy of the Omega calendar of events. This was on Thursday. There was a Jean Houston workshop listed there to be held that weekend!

"Oh, wow!" I got excited. "I have to go!"

My friend looked at me kindly. "Don't count on it. She's no doubt fully sold out. Her workshops are

VERY popular." Not to be discouraged, I dialled the number in the calendar.

The voice on the phone sounded a little bit apologetic as she looked up her list of participants and said, "I'm afraid there's only one single seat remaining."

"Perfect!" I exclaimed and gave her my credit card number. My friend printed a map off the computer for me, and I was off and running!

I picked up my diabetic medical kit and a few changes of clothes, hopped in my car, and drove to the border that night. The next morning, I crossed the border and made my way through the mountain and lake country of northern New York State, one winding road after another. (Has anyone ever taught you that a short cut should really be called a "long and winding cut"?)

I arrived at the campus about 10 minutes before the first session was to begin. I signed in, grabbed a cabin key, and dropped my bag in the main office, promising to pick it up if we had a break. And that was the start of my long and treasured adventure with Jean Houston.

Teacher, healer, scholar, guide, counsellor, friend ... she has played many a role in my life since that first meeting. I would say she captures best a description of her work in the world when she refers to herself as a "midwife of souls." Amen to that!

The year 2000 AD wove several new storylines into my life. I'd now had a year of Mystery School Weekends under my belt. These workshops had awakened a sleeping giant–size yearning in my inner life. Finally! An adventure where I had community while exploring the depths of all levels of understanding.

I also yearned for a loving human companion and, during this year, found a man who I was later to marry. Third time lucky! (Or so I hoped.) Martyn attended an introductory weekend with Jean Houston, not long after we met. She offered an introduction to "Entelechy" that weekend, and Martyn seemed to get a lot out of that, which made me happy. I couldn't imagine being with someone who just wanted me to be "ordinary." My intention was to work toward being *extraordinary*!

We enjoyed the summer together, sailing on the lake in his 22-foot sailboat, participating in local theatre on and off stage. I had my golf, and he was a remote control aircraft enthusiast, who joined a local flying club. We lived about an hour apart down the highway but enjoyed lots of time together at one place or the other.

Then, I had a visit with my medical doctor, which threw a wrinkle (or should I say a hurdle?) into this pleasant picture.

KIDNEY SISTERS

I cannot write about the gifts to be found with golf buddies without mentioning my most remarkable experience with a friendship established on the golf course. In the year 2000, I was told by my doctor that I would soon have to go on dialysis and be put on the waiting list for a kidney transplant. Since I have no relatives who would qualify as a donor, I could expect to be on dialysis for a few years before finding an appropriate cadaver match.

My golf buddies (with whom I played at least weekly if not more often) detected my sombre mood that day, and I told them what the doctor had said.

One of our fearsome foursome stepped forward, clear-eyed and sounding very sure of her words, and said, "You can have one of mine!"

When I recovered my voice, I said, "Oh Edith, that is an amazing offer, but this is no small thing! We're talking major surgery. I think you better sleep on it."

She replied, "I'll sleep on it if you want, but I know what I can do." The next morning, she phoned me and said, "Okay, I slept. Now what do we do first?"

The answer to that question was blood and tissue tests, and then antibody tests to establish whether or not Edith could be a possible donor.

As we walked into the lab, I pointed to her right kidney and joked, "I want THAT one ... IT looks feisty!" We just laughed.

Lo and behold, we had the same blood type, matching tissue type, and compatible antibodies. There was only one antibody that Edith had that I was missing and that could be rectified with medications for me post-transplant if we got that far. We are only a year apart in age, and most surprising was that we were a two-out-of-six genetic match. That's even better than some siblings!

We continued the testing and preparations at Toronto General Hospital with a series of other tests, both physical and psychological. We laughed together over some of the questions the psychologist had asked Edith.

Doctor: What would you do if you gave your friend your kidney, and she neglected to take care of it properly with diet, medications, and such?

Edith: What would you like me to do? Tie a string to it so that if she doesn't behave, I can yank it back?

It didn't take the doctor long to check off on his form that she was in a very healthy mental and emotional state!

The surgery was tentatively scheduled for later the same year. The final testing was a series of three 24-hour urine collection tests. After so much success, it was hard to accept that the first of those tests came back showing high amounts of protein in Edith's urine. That could indicate problems with Edith's kidney health, and it did not allow us to proceed with our hoped for schedule. Repeated tests showed the same.

With high hopes of being able to have a transplant before the end of the year, the doctors had put off my dialysis to prepare for more immediate surgery. However, it seemed that it was not to be, and I proceeded quickly to dialysis.

Dialysis was to be provided at Orillia Soldiers' Memorial Hospital, which was closer to my home. I soon saw a kidney specialist there who installed the port in my jugular vein so the treatments could begin. The jugular port would be temporary since I had decided to opt for Continuous Ambulatory Peritoneal Dialysis rather than attending to the hospital several times a week. CAPD is more portable than hemodialysis, and I hoped for more freedom with that choice.

Meanwhile, Edith had gone with her husband to their winter home in Florida. We were both disappointed, but I certainly didn't want her taking undue risk with her own kidneys to provide one for me.

Martyn, still in the picture, was supportive and kind throughout my struggles with all of this. I certainly thought I had found a keeper. He even agreed for the next year to accompany me to and from Jean Houston's Mystery School in New York.

For those weekends, I certainly couldn't be considered a light packer. We would drive down with a trunk full of the equipment and supplies it took to do the dialysis. I stopped whatever we were doing, on the highway or at the camp, to do my dialysis four times a day for about 45 minutes each time.

The community at Mystery School was a loving, healing, safety net for me and made a world of difference in my overall well-being. At one of the weekends, I was the centre of a group healing ceremony designed to call my kidney home.

After that ceremony, it seemed that destiny itself was shifted. A total of four friends, both from within the community and outside of it, were tested as a potential donor. There were at least two potential matches for me, though none as good a match as Edith had seemed to be.

In the summer of 2001, Edith, getting ready for her yearly migration back to Canada, called me on the phone. She told me she had taken the winter to really consider it and wanted to know if it was okay with me if she tried again to be considered as a donor. She had consulted with a kidney specialist, who had agreed with her that the Atkins Diet (a high-protein diet popular at the time) could have caused the unfortunate urine test results. She wanted to take another run at it without the Atkins Diet. Edith said she just KNEW that she was supposed to do this, but she would back off if I was uncomfortable with it.

It was essential to my sense of ethics, as well as legal ethics when it comes to transplant laws, that one does not solicit a kidney from another person. We spoke at some length and decided that if the specialists, after repeating the urine tests, felt it was safe, then I would trust her "knowing" sense to direct her course.

Jean Houston had helped me understand how knowing goes well beyond logic or caution, or even intelligence, and must be listened to.

At the end of August 2001, after a year of progress and delays, ups and downs, Edith gave me the gift of Life, all wrapped up in a healthy, vigorous kidney. Now, years later, we get together on the golf course. We still enjoy a laugh together out there. I'm certain that I would not be breathing, much less golfing, if not for my buddy.

Edith usually beats me by just a few strokes—and yes, we are both playing the best we can. We wouldn't have it any other way.

WILLY WHOOPS!

I wanted to give my new kidney a name. Edith's other given name, is Wilhelmina, so I named the kidney Willy. A few days after surgery, when I was able to go for short walks down the hall, I caused a bit of a commotion. I am sorry that Edith was not permitted to be my roommate in the hospital, or we'd have laughed ourselves silly over this incident. Let me tell you what happened.

I got carefully out of my bed, picking up my Gucci bag (as I referred to my urine collection pouch), and shuffled around the bed to get my shawl (a healing shawl I had been given at Mystery School) and my walker on wheels parked on that side of my bed. As almost an afterthought, I stood on tiptoe to reach for my golf cap (with "Goddess" on the front of the cap—just for fun).

When I reached for it, I felt a strong tug and then heard a *snap* ... and saw urine spraying all over the place from between my legs! I started to whoop out loud and for a minute just kept whooping. This started my roommate whooping as well! (She did not speak English, but I guess I had no such excuse.)

I hauled my gown up to take a look, afraid that I had yanked the catheter right out of my body! But no, there was about six inches of brown rubber tubing, flapping around like a fire hose gone crazy! I grabbed hold of the tube and stood there like that, surrounded by soggy sheets and a puddle.

The nurse came running, assessed the situation, and finally said, "Oh My God!! You really DO have a Willy!" We all started laughing … and she brought me a bucket.

SETTING SAIL

In recognition of my need for freedom of travel and celebrating life, I asked one of the senior kidney specialists how long after the transplant (if all went well) I'd have to stay near the hospital until the schedule of post-transplant testing would be down to fewer than once a week. (I have always resisted being on a short leash for any length of time.)

The specialist estimated that at about 13 weeks I'd only have to visit the lab every two weeks rather than weekly. I nodded and immediately set about booking a Caribbean cruise for week 14.

Martyn's son and daughter-in–law, and their son (I think he was four or five) travelled with us on that trip. It was a very enjoyable celebration of still being alive!

During that cruise, Mart bought for me a blue topaz ring, which evolved into an engagement ring as we talked about our future. He had been so kind and loving, and I was quite smitten with him, so I thought that, in spite of my other unfortunate endings, I should *"seize the day!"* and give it one more try.

We planned a wedding for the following summer. We had two ceremonies—the first performed by Jean Houston at one of the Mystery School weekend gatherings and the second with friends and family on Lake Muskoka.

Sadly, although we had an exceptional start to our time together, lasting happiness was not in our cards. It is not my intention here to appoint myself judge and jury, find fault for any failed relationships, or say whether or not they were mistakes. Mart and I had a good run for a while but, as I got stronger (with the benefit of a healthy kidney) and our life's surroundings and occupations changed, we were thrown into an unrecoverable tailspin, resulting eventually in disappointment with each other. The bruising of the heart that ensued was a tough price to pay. One can only hope that what is paid for becomes lasting wisdom.

In any case, our marriage ended in 2008. In the meantime, life had certainly not been uneventful. There was even a brief but intense love in the aftermath. I'd like to think I've learned that legal entanglement is neither a guarantee of love, nor of learning, nor of leaving.

MY MYTHING GREEK

I recognized in you, my beloved,
my creative partner, playmate of the cosmos,
trusted friend, evokateur, protector
and love mate of my soul.

You recognized me, Queen Bee,
kookla, glika, goddess, teacher,
and absolutely a-d-o-r-a-b-l-e.

You brought forth in me,
a depth of LOVE that I had never
felt before, filling my heart, my soul,
my thoughts and my body, with
rich and unconditional floods of light.
You inspired me to overflow ...

You asked me once what would cause me
the greatest pain, and I answered
you honestly.
And then you did exactly as I had described.
You tore away the flesh that holds my
heart ...
And still I love you.

You tried to burn me in the fire of
your entrapment.
In attempting to fight the white bull,
fight off the chains that you felt restrict-
ing your very life,
I was included in the sacrifice; the bull and
I, together.

For a brief, oh so sweet time, SOMEone,
someone living inside of you
made me feel loved,
overflowing with the light and rapture
of LOVE.
Yet somehow you seemed to be able to turn
your love
on and off like a switch ...
and still, I love you.

HOME, RECLAIMED, RENEWED

Lighting a candle here and there
I wander through my freedom lair
smelling lilac on the air
and "lightness of being" everywhere.

The threat has passed, the morning light
bounces merrily through the hall
and tiny rainbow splash reflections
decorate my kitchen wall.

There are colours I've not seen before.
Furnishings and flooring tiles,
which sat so long without expression,
now are sporting whimsical smiles.

A sheltered patio beckons me "Sit."
I contemplate my newfound world
I've wriggled out of my cocoon
and wondrous wings have now unfurled.

This space has become welcoming
It opens its arms, invites me in,
and all the trees surrounding the house
are waltzing in the summer wind.

Would you like to visit me?
In my nest here in the trees?
You could play here, you could rest,
The air will lift you up, you'll see ...

And soon you'll find your voice has changed
it laughs and speaks in gentler tones
Your lungs expand with sweetened air
and carefree energies fill your bones.

You offer blessings to this house,
anointing each room with basil and dreams
only to find in the magic of opening
The castle within you is more than it
seemed ...

Lower your drawbridge, let hope in,
We'll float through aerial space and time
creating "home" and love, and sacred
space within your heart and mine.

A TIME FOR REBALANCING

Several seasons passed, with me living in the house we had shared, taking time to cleanse my wounds, re-centring the place around a more positive environment for my growing appreciation of gifts received and miracles observed.

One of the first changes I made to the house was to purchase a canopy for the back deck on the upper level. That deck was a beloved perch for me. I've always thought I'd live in a treehouse—at least until brought to my senses each year by our enthusiastically frosty Canadian winters! This house allowed me the closest possible illusion of such a place, and I delayed downsizing to a more sensible and affordable house to enjoy at least one complete cycle of seasons there among the treetops.

I continued to study and travel with Jean, when possible, enjoying the exploration of the larger world and the company of fellow explorers on our inner and outer journeys. I continued to be involved in singing, becoming a part (baritone) in a women's barbershop quartet. Own Accord sang together for the simple joy of making music together, and we did fairly well competitively in our regional competitions.

The golf course I had worked on with my dad gradually grew. I am proud of the team of contributors to the club's growth and the administration of this unique offering in private club golf.

AUTUMN COLOUR

A splash of colour Crimson, Gold,
All hues of Autumn Splendour

Cascading down to dampened ground
A rustling path to render

To kick and shluff along with feet
In sturdy walking shoes

Reminiscent of child's play
In the forests of my youth.

Deep Breath and into Winter
Soon enough we'll trudge through snow.

Autumn stay a little longer
Fill my heart before you go …

CROSS OVER THE BRIDGE

The song "Cross Over the Bridge," made famous by Patti Page in the mid-1950s, was one of the songs that my dad used to sing with the band at the golf club where I grew up.

Half a century later, it was my great privilege, and a pivotal moment in my life, to be with Dad when his time came to actually cross over. Dad had suffered an aneurysm in the artery leading to one of his kidneys in November 2002.

I received the news over the phone in my hospital room in Toronto, where I was being treated for an infection that was threatening my newly transplanted kidney. Dad was being transported to a different hospital where a specialist had been found who could operate immediately on him. Getting out of my hospital bed to be with him was simply out of the question.

My mom went with him to the assigned hospital, staying with him as he waited to go into the OR for his surgery. The surgeon came to the side of his gurney to speak to him and, among other things, told him that he had about a 10 percent chance of surviving his time on the table. I was later told that Dad just looked him in the eye and said, "Well then, you'd better do your best work, hadn't you?" The surgeon nodded his agreement and then went to prepare for the task at hand.

In the meantime, Dad looked at his wife of more than 50 years and said, "Whatever happens ... we're in this together. Right?"

She replied with a definite, "Right!" and it was time for him to go into surgery.

In my hospital room across the city, I was painfully aware of how awful it must be for her, waiting for the outcome. I was talking to a dear family friend about the situation, and he could not tolerate the idea that she was alone with all it. He drove over to sit with her in the waiting room and lend his support. Angels do indeed come in many shapes and sizes.

Dad beat the odds and was in the ICU for weeks after his surgery. He was conscious but somewhat confused and distressed, and Mom would not leave his side. Once released from my hospital, I drove down to see him and tried to keep Mom supplied with whatever she might need, since she was not going to go home until he was much better.

After he reached a more or less stable status, the decision was made to transfer my dad to the local hospital nearer to where they lived. That should have been an improvement, but sadly, the ambulance doing the transfer got into an accident—the driver was trying to avoid hitting a dog in the road.

In the back of the vehicle, Dad was thrown forward in the gurney and got badly jostled. The attendant in the back jumped out to see if the dog could be helped. My mom was livid.

They did get Dad to the destination later that evening, but during the night, he suffered a stroke. In fact, he suffered at least two strokes in the next few days.

After the second stroke, on one particular morning I'll not likely forget, I was standing beside Dad's bed with Mom beside me at his head, and my son to my left near his feet, facing the door.

A senior doctor at the hospital came into the room, took a look at Dad's chart then put it back at the bottom of the bed. He walked over toward Mom, gave her a perfunctory pat on the shoulder, and said, "Not much to hope for here, Beth."

She barely paid him any mind, and my son and I both went cold at what we saw as a terrible thing for him to have said. As the doctor was leaving the room, I looked down at Dad. He had not uttered a word since his stroke and was hardly "present" at all. Or so everybody thought.

I said to him, in the same tone we had always used when enjoying a confidence or a joke, "We're not done yet, are we?"

Dad just grunted out a derisive "harrumph."

I assured him. "Well, if YOU are not quitting ... WE are not quitting!!" What followed was a long hospital stay, and two and a half years of stalwart and determined effort on my mom's part to keep him going and try to ensure he had the best quality of life possible.

During that time, he was mostly at home. She arranged for a hospital bed in their bedroom. Orthodox as well as alternative medical care was provided. She would feed him and keep him clean and as comfortable as possible.

She hired a care worker to assist so he could stay at home. Dad was included in social and other situations to the greatest extent possible. If it was a formal occasion, Mom would help him don his tux and take him along. At this point, he could walk with assistance, and he'd stand at "cocktail hour" with a wine glass full of ginger ale, or whatever non-alcoholic beverage was available, in one hand and grin at people who came over to say, "Hi."

He might say, "Hi, Chief. How are you doing?" He was rarely able to remember their names, but he enjoyed seeing them and being a part of the occasion.

He could not be left alone. Even at night, when he had been asleep, he could not get up to go to the bathroom without help, though he'd try. He'd forget he needed help and fall to the floor in the bedroom.

He had a durable sense of humour and spirit. During one of his hospital stays, his long-time friend Bert visited. Bert had recently had knee surgery and, although he was up walking, he was still somewhat sore from it. The visit consisted mostly of Bert telling stories, and Dad watching him and listening intently, but saying nothing.

When it was time to go, Bert said, "I better go, Mac. Jeez, it's a long walk back to the car."

Dad blinked at him and said, "You don't have to walk … you can run if you like."

The other style of communication that seemed to get through to Dad was music. The songs of his youth and his years singing with the band seemed to reach him most effectively. This came to light after his stroke and during his hospital stay.

It was morning, and the technician from the hospital lab had come to get a blood sample from Dad's arm, as was the routine. One of the effects of his stroke seemed to be that the right side of my dad's body had become like a black hole in his awareness. He didn't like being turned to the right or to have anyone approach him from that side or move him in that direction.

When the lab tech tried to take his blood from his right arm, Dad struggled and tried to pull away. He was distressed, and I could see that getting blood from that arm was going to be futile.

I thought, *I've got to find a way to distract him!* I leaned toward him at his left side and said, "Dad, can you help me?"

He turned his face to me. "Huh?"

I began to sing, "I love coffee, I love tea ..." Dad chimed in and continued the song ... IN TUNE and with all the right words! "...I love the Java Jive and it loves me!" By the time we finished the song, the lab tech had finished her task and peace was restored.

In the spring of 2005, my friend Edith and I decided to take a few days to travel to North Carolina, play golf, and visit some dear friends. The morning after we arrived, my mom was on the phone saying I'd better get home because she didn't think Dad would last much longer. He'd taken a turn for the worse, and she was at the Uxbridge Hospital. This was a smaller hospital with a smaller patient population. Mom felt he would likely get more personal care without the tension and hubbub of a larger city hospital.

That morning, Edith drove me to the Myrtle Beach airport, and I flew to Toronto and drove to where Mom was sitting at his bedside. He was noticeably weaker than the last time I'd seen him. Pale, almost grey-skinned, so very thin, and not breathing easily at all. Mom, as she had done before, refused to leave his room. My son Jason and I spent as much time as we could in the room with them. Dad's godson, Brock, came to see him during the week.

During these very challenging times, Mom's brother, Bud, had also been coping with his own medical challenges. He had suffered colon cancer in the last few years, and although Mom was very tied up with Dad's care, she made a point of at least checking in with him by phone when he had doctor's appointments, or sometimes just to see how he was doing.

The day that Brock came to visit Dad, Mom was upset. She had been unable to reach Bud by phone for a couple of days and was really worried about him. She was determined not to leave Dad, though, and felt torn. I offered to go and check on Bud, and she agreed, though she was worried about me taking that on when we were all so focused on and concerned about Dad. I asked Brock if he would drive down to Bud's house with me, and he readily agreed.

When we arrived at Bud's house, I went up to the front door and knocked. I didn't get an answer so I went toward the back of the house. On the way, I tried to look through the side window to see if he was inside watching TV. Uncle Bud was hard of hearing and could well have been unable to hear the knock on the door with a television turned on.

I wasn't quite tall enough to see in, though, so Brock came over to have a look. Meanwhile, I walked around to the back door thinking it might not be locked. As I rounded the corner, I saw him. Bud was lying inert, face down in the garden beside the back door.

My hand flew to my mouth, and I whispered, "Oh, Bud."

Brock, seeing my expression, came to where I stood and saw Bud lying there. He moved quickly to him, handing me his cell phone as he passed by. He told me to call 911 as he turned Bud's body face up to check for signs of life.

The police were there quickly. It was obvious to us all that there was no "saving" to be done. Bud had probably not drawn a breath for at least a couple of days. The dealings with the police and medical examiner, and communication of necessary contact and funeral home information was all done within an hour ... and Bud's body was taken away in a hearse.

Brock, obviously shaken by what he'd just dealt with, nevertheless treated me with kindness and concern, and drove me back up to the Uxbridge Hospital. My mom, her husband struggling to stay alive beside her, must now be informed that her only brother, my Uncle Bud, had died, alone, just outside of his own back door.

That was on Good Friday at Easter that year. My dad passed away the following Wednesday.

The morning of my dad's passing, I came into the room to find Mom somewhat agitated. When I asked her what was happening, she explained, "He's really struggling today, and I don't know what to do." I was silent.

Then she added, "I usually shave him every morning. He just hates to go unshaven. I can't get at his face though. He's kind of turned to the side, and I don't want to hurt him."

I watched her dilemma for a few seconds then finally said, "Look, if the thing you both are used to is for you to shave him each morning ... then you should shave him. I can hold his head. It won't hurt him, I promise."

Mom followed me with the shaving kit as I went over to his bed. Shoving the bed away from the wall a bit, I climbed up onto the mattress above his pillow and held Dad's head in the same way I would hold someone to do Reiki energy healing.

Cradling his head in my hands, my thumbs gently resting on his scalp, I could feel his pulse beating under my touch. I watched as she ever so gently moistened the brush, lathered his face and drew his safety razor across and up over his skin to shave him. When she was finished, she carefully wiped his face clean and softly patted him on his chest as if to say "There, that's better."

I felt that there was something he was waiting for. Mom noticed my hesitation and asked, "What?"

I replied that there were things I wanted to say to him, but I didn't want to upset her in the process.

She told me, "Say what you need to say."

I spoke out loud, then, telling him that, although we would miss him very much and loved him so very much, that we would get along somehow. We had learned everything he had taught us and if he needed to go now, it was okay. We would be okay. He could let go.

As I was speaking, I found myself in a deeper state of mind in which I could actually see a bridge stretching out in front of him and me. We seemed to move forward together tentatively onto that bridge until I saw a couple of figures up ahead on the other side of the bridge. I spoke again.

"Oh look, your mother is waiting for you … and Rob is there too! Your mother will take good care of you … and Rob? If anyone tried to do you wrong, he'd soon stop them. You will be fine. Everything will be all right. You can go across now. You can let go."

As my voice faded into quiet, so did the pulse under my hands. I felt his pulse slow … and then stop. He took one weak breath, and then he was gone.

I stayed very still until I felt he had crossed. Then I looked at Mom, still with her hand lightly on his chest, and said, "Do you want to be alone with him for a bit?"

She nodded, and I carefully let go of his head and got off the bed. My son was standing at the opposite side of the bed from Mom, and we went outside the room.

116

"We just need to hold the space for them for a bit," I said, and he nodded his assent, understanding completely.

A couple of weeks later ...

During that Easter season, my dad passed, Uncle Bud (an avid golfer) passed, and the gentleman, Ray Whaley, who had done much of the shaping of golf courses on his bulldozer for my dad, passed as well. Dad must have sent us a blessing of a humorous thought. It is a common question among golfers as to whether or not there are golf courses in Heaven. We had to agree. If there were not any before, there certainly would be some NOW!

July 15, 2003
Vespra Hills Golf Club
Opening Day!
Mac Frost hits off the
first tee to open the course

YOU'RE UP AFTER MAC!

In June of 2003, I was finishing up the last things we needed to do before opening the course near Barrie the next month. I went to visit Mom and Dad's house, one day, and asked Mom her opinion on something I wasn't sure about.

In the past, whenever Dad had built and opened a golf course, he had a ritual of hitting the first ball off the tee. Now, we were readying the course for opening ... but Dad was only able to walk with a walker and couldn't get out of bed without help. He seemed not to understand a lot of what went on around him.

I didn't know whether to tell him we were almost ready to open, or whether it might break his heart to be unable to be there for his customary ritual.

Mom said, "You better tell him. If he finds out later and realizes that he wasn't told, he'll be VERY upset. Just go tell him. He may or may not remember or understand anyway."

Mom's advice made sense to me, and I went into the bedroom to talk to my dad.

His face perked up. "Hi. What are you doing?"

"I just came for a visit, and I wanted to talk to you," I said.

Dad sat up a bit and looked at me with that wide-eyed stare that meant he was paying attention. I told him things were going well at the golf course and it would soon be time to open it. He seemed to consider that carefully.

"How long?" he asked.

"Until we open?" He nodded and listened intently. "We're aiming at mid-July. It's about three weeks from now."

"Three weeks!" he exclaimed, an expression of amazement on his face. After a pause, he said, "Okay." Then he seemed to get lost in his own thoughts and waved good-bye to me, so I left the room.

When the day came, Mom phoned to ask if this was the day we wanted to open. When I confirmed it, she said that they'd be coming up directly. Sure enough, before much time had passed, I saw her car coming up the driveway. I hollered at the rest of the crew to come with me and ran down to the driveway beside the first tee.

Much to my surprise, Dad stepped out of the passenger side of the car without extra help! He was wearing his golf shoes, slacks, a golf jacket, and his favourite Sam Snead–style golf hat! He began a quick-paced shuffle toward the first tee.

I looked on, astonished, then went to Mom and asked, "Have you got his driver with you?" She'd put his golf bag in the trunk. I got out his driver and ran to catch up with him. Dad was still doing the Tim Conway Shuffle toward the tee and had almost reached it. He was standing between the markers when I caught up with him and handed him his club.

Dad grinned at me and nodded a gesture of thanks. Slowly, he tugged at the club cover and then tossed it to me, just as he had been doing for years.

By this time, Mom and some of the crew were standing by the side of the tee. His gallery. He took a golf stance and began to waggle the club near the ball.

Mom and I grinned, and I said to one of the guys, "Get a picture of this, will you?" Then, quite suddenly, the picture changed. Dad firmed up his stance. He began tapping the club behind the ball and tried to straighten up his left arm. A look of fierce determination and focus came into his face. Mom and I looked at each other with concerned amazement.

I thought to myself, *Oh my God. He'll take a full swing, and it might just be the end of him!* Just as quickly, the thought followed that if he had to die ... that would probably be his first choice of the way to go.

He took the biggest swing he could, and as we all watched in awe, he hit the ball into the air and 140 yards down the fairway. He turned to grin at us. We all cheered! It was certainly not as long a drive as he might have envisioned but pretty darn miraculous for the condition he was in.

I was shocked. My mouth agog. "Oh my God, Dad! Can you do that again?"

He turned to me, grinned, and got that look on his face that seemed to say *that's a silly question*. Then he raised his eyebrows and, in an ironic tone, said, "Have you got another ball?"

Gary, one of the greens crew, ran down the fairway to retrieve the ball. After Dad took a couple more swings for the photo op, he handed me his club and started to make his way back to the car. I thanked him and told him I was REALLY proud of him. He settled into the car seat and Mom drove him back home. She reported to me later that he slept for the rest of that day and the next as well. It is said that the biggest rule of living a full life is to simply Show Up.

He certainly did that ... in spades.

MAC'S MAPLE

("You can't *BUY* a thing like that!")

Today, I stood beside the ninth tee on the golf course, looking up at the grand old tree we call Mac's Maple. I was contemplating the best possible way to preserve its majesty and historical value as we stepped into the next phase of development at Vespra Hills.

Dave Caldwell is my greens superintendent and co-creator in many of the projects I'm inclined to jump into at the club. Dave and I were figuring out her girth, height, and weight. We were trying to come up with the best method of moving the tree from the place where she has stood for untold numbers of years to the clubhouse, which is to be built in the near future.

In the 1990s, when the building of the course was taking place, this tree was a favourite of my dad's (Mac Frost). He went to considerable trouble to avoid injuring the tree in his design and construction of the course.

Every year, he would drive out to that spot on the land with me and say, "Look at that maple. Isn't that a BEAUT! You can't *buy* a thing like that." The tree would reward his gaze with a resplendent display of brilliant red leaves, bursting with the energy that only radiant colour and transitioning life can engender.

Well, it would seem that the admiration and affection may have been mutual. When Dad passed on in the spring of 2005, the tree also began to show signs of fatigue. I invited an arborist to come and visit, and he agreed with other experts that the beautiful old maple was on her way out. There was no hope of keeping the tree alive and flourishing.

Looking up at the sky, I said out loud, "What? You liked it so much that you took her with you??"

I invited out a small group of dear friends and fellow tree huggers to acknowledge her significance with a ritual involving sage, song, and spirit, and began to prepare to say good-bye to the old tree that had brought Dad so much pleasure.

Now, I'm sure he was not the maple's first admirer. My mom actually grew up on the property, as did my Uncle Bud, and I suspect that at least one of them must have climbed up in her ample branches, along with who knows how many visitors to the property over the years.

I simply was not prepared to resign her to becoming firewood. So, I got to thinking that I'd like to have her stand (or at least her main trunk and branches, properly preserved and re-enforced) as representative of the history and evolution of this place. I'd like to have her stand, like a family tree, or perhaps as a symbol of reaching for higher levels, in the 35-foot high entrance of our new clubhouse, here, on the property she has graced since long before I came along.

I fervently hope the old girl will continue to be a thought-provoking and beautiful reminder of life's journey. My dreams are climbing her branches now. Her trunk still appears sturdy enough to handle it.

Yes, Mac's Maple stands proudly in the north foyer of the building. I like to think Dad would enjoy this tribute.

Mac's Maple Then

Mac's Maple Now

DEAD HEADING

"Be sure to cut those heads off
once the bloom is finished,"
Mother said.
"The plant will thank you for it
in the Spring."

So, looking forward to the
gratitude of Irises and Lilies,
I did what I was told.

Slowly walking through the perennial garden,
snipping and clutching the severed stems,
feeling the moisture of the recent rain
captured in the dried husks of petals
now running down my arm.

"Thank you," I said to the Irises.
"Thank you," to the Lilies.
In both their beauty, now fading,
and the pleasure and communion
of this simple task of renewal,
they had shown me much to be grateful for.

And they and I will honour
each other yet again,
come Spring.

CHECKING THE REARVIEW MIRROR

In 2008, my marriage to Martyn came to an end. What had started as a sense of soul-deep kinship, when subjected to significant lifestyle and role changes, did not hold up. In his response to my challenges during the kidney transplant, he had been kind and supportive. In the idyllic setting of our life in Muskoka, we had enjoyed a lovely time of balance.

However, then Dad's illness and subsequent passing pulled at me to move down closer to the golf course project. I was taking on a demanding role, trying to further Dad's legacy at the course. Martyn ended up taking on the role of homemaker, and we evidently were not as able to find a balance between us. What differences there were in our desires and intentions became glaringly obvious to us, and we ended up negotiating a parting of the ways. He moved to a new house a few minutes' drive away. This was hard.

I thought, at the time, that we both felt deeply sorry that this was how we finished. Within a couple of weeks of leaving our home, however, Martyn was co-habiting with a friend from our Muskoka days. Did I learn anything? I learned it's important to resolve that I would never again try to make myself lesser to reassure a partner of his superiority. It was time to rediscover who I was.

THE UNFOLDING OF MYSTERIES

Over the next several years, even though much was happening on the golf course project, I was blessed with the opportunity and freedom to travel with Jean Houston and members of the Mystery School community.

There were two trips to Egypt. One trip to "Renaissance Italy" and two different trips to Greece. Not to mention, time spent on the big island of Hawaii! Jean focused her journeys with us on the ancient sites and natural wonders. Spiritual and mind-expanding explorations were abundant! These travels were FUN as much as they were ENLIGHTENING.

Let me share with you a story of what happened on one of our trips to Egypt, in November of 2008. We were in the capable hands of Quest Travel and our guides, Sameh and Emil. We also enjoyed the benefits of Jean's long-time friendship with Zahir Havaas, who was the Egyptian authority over antiquities and could therefore gain us access to sites that might otherwise have been denied a group of tourists.

One fine morning, it was a 4:30 wake-up call, breakfast until 5:15, and then off to the West Bank. We had an amazing visit to the Valley of the Kings planned. One of our guides, Emil, had been the head of security for the Valley for some years and was known there. We arrived and entered long before it opened to the public.

We visited a tomb that was fairly well known, and then Emil said to Jean, "There is a tomb here that I want you and your group to come and activate ... it has been asleep for a long time ... please come and be in this place."

We quickly scurried after him to another opening in the Valley. We walked back into the tomb, through a couple of larger vestibule chambers, and then into the sanctuary in the very back of the excavation. Our way back into the tomb was lit by a sparse string of white lights—like Christmas lights but few and far between.

Deep inside was the holiest space of the temple. Here, we gathered around a ceremonial sarcophagus and began to chant the "Shanti" (peace). Having experimented with different vocal placements in other tombs, I sang the Shanti through the upper resonance chambers of my face, around the eyes, sinuses, and forward spaces, knowing it would sound more resonant in the temple and roll through the space.

As we chanted, the lights suddenly went dark. None of us broke the sound of our chant. We chanted on in the dark as ONE with full sound and reverence. After about five minutes (I'm guessing at the time—the whole thing became rather timeless), the lights came back on and we closed off the chant.

I opened my eyes and was wonderstruck by what I saw next. I gazed around the sanctuary at the carvings on the walls and realized that I could see them clearly. Not just the basic, but every detail, in all its colour and glory! I was awestruck by the sight. I had not seen so clearly for years! (Having had multiple surgeries on my retinas as well as cataract surgery—this had become a physical reality for me.) SUDDENLY I COULD SEE!

Jean had gathered up the altar cloth she'd used at the centre of our ceremony and was moving forward along the path to the opening of the tomb. I hurried to catch up with her, and tugging on her sleeve, exclaimed, "Jean! I can see!"

She nodded and smiled. I grabbed her arm and with more urgency said, "No, Jean! You didn't hear me! I can SEE! I haven't had clear vision for YEARS! I can SEE!"

The urgency of what I was saying clicked, and Jean grabbed the back of my head, pointing my eyes toward the beautiful coloured carvings of gods, goddesses, pharaohs, and such that adorned all the walls around us.

"LOOK!" she insisted. "REALLY SEE THEM ALL!"

She then grabbed my hand and signalled to the group to follow us as she led me into one of the larger vestibules near the entrance. She signalled Peggy, saying that we must sing! We all began to sing Pachelbel's Canon. I sang at the top of my lungs ... we all did. I was crying for JOY and overcome with the sense of being part of a miracle.

After a few repeats of the music, one of our guides peeked into the doorway of the vestibule. He signalled to Jean that it was time for us to leave. We gradually brought the singing to a close and made our way out of the opening into the desert sunshine. As I walked outside, I looked up at the top of the mountain ridge that surrounded the Valley of the Kings.

The sky was the most intense blue I'd ever seen. The top ridge of the mountain was a CLEAR sharp line against the sky. As I walked back toward where our buses were parked, local people stared at me. I felt that I must be glowing as I walked. Some even came up to me to shyly touch the hem of my garments.

My vision and my faith had been powerfully reinforced and renewed. My realization and gratitude for the power of the connection between spirit, mind, and body, further confirmed.

AN IRISH BLESSING

A gaggle of friends (some familiar, some new ones), my son Jason, and I travelled together in the central western part of Ireland. We were led in our journey of adventures by Gerry and Denise Dignan. Our travels became a "Magical Musical Mystery Tour".

I'd had the pleasure of getting to know Gerry and Denise as the musical and dance leaders in the community of Jean Houston's Mystery School in New York State. We visited such sites as Bridget's cave, Galway Bay, shrines and local museums, a lovely cave where the leprechauns were known to hang out, and a number of pubs where we would sing and carouse with the best of 'em!

One evening, after checking into a new hotel, a few of us, including the jovial bus driver who had escorted us safely along the winding roads of the countryside in our big, comfortable chariot, retired for a wee nip in the hotel bar before heading off to bed for the night.

Being a fan of Scotch when I occasionally take a drink, nothing would do but that I taste a dram of Irish Whiskey to properly compare the two. A very pleasant night cap, indeed!

Retiring to my hotel room, I settled in for the night. Taking my usual medications and other nightly rituals,

I soon fell into a deep and welcome slumber, having had a full day of fresh air and fun. In my dreams (or so I thought), I found myself floating just under the surface of a deep indigo-coloured ocean. I imagined I must be feeling the way a whale would, suspended beneath the surface, though not too far below. Every now and then, my body would float up and break the surface, and feeling the air upon my face, I would suck in a deep breath. Then, slowly exhaling, I would submerge again to my level of buoyancy a few feet below.

A few times, I rose up and then down again, gently bouncing on the currents and swells of the sea. In one such surfacing, I realized that I was physically wet. The bed was soaked with my own perspiration, and I felt that I had slipped the bonds of conscious presence in my physical body.

Noting this state of being, I slipped below the water once again and was greeted by a luminous gift—a depth of peace and joy I had not felt before or after. In that moment, in my altered awareness, I realized I was being given a choice. Oh! How wonderful! A choice. Delivered with a kiss of bliss. I realized I could choose to continue living on this plane of existence that we share, or I could choose to simply slip away. Slip away to a place of no responsibilities, no pain, no guilt, nothing to do or be. A simple and complete state of blissful love. I considered letting go. Ahhh ... so tempting.

A thought then nudged my comprehension. A thought of my son. If I left in this way, at this time, then he would surely have a sorrowful mess on his hands. That was not an acceptable outcome, and it stirred me to action. Coming up to the surface once more, I reached for the glucose tablets I keep at my bedside.

As a diabetic of many years, it's a habit that was usual for me. However, I found I could only move one arm; the rest of my body seemed inert. I was unable to locate the glucose container. I knew I needed help but struggled to conceptualize how to get that help.

I exhaled into the depth and rose to try again. This time, the thought struck me, *telephone*, which seemed a good idea, but then I didn't know what number to call. On the next surfacing, I thought, *Zero. There's always somebody at Zero.* Reaching for the phone on the nightstand, I was unable to pull it toward me. I fumbled around until I was able to press zero.

A delightful, young, Irish-accented voice said, "Good evening, Ma'am [pronounced like Mum], what can I do for ye then?"

Oh my, I thought, *What do I tell him? How do I explain myself?* Finally, out of a groggy mouth, I said, "Sh-sh-sugar. I need sh-sh-sugar. Diabetic."

"I see," he said thoughtfully. "Have you had your insulin, then?"

"Oh gawd, don't give me that! It'll kill me. Need sugar!"

"Right, Mum," he said and hung up the phone.

I submerged once again. The next thing I was aware of was a young Irish lad, tall and dark with a curly mop of hair, and three bottles held carefully in his arm.

"Will you be having some of this then?" he asked.

"Sh-sh-sh-got sh-shugar?" I asked, slurring terribly.

"Oh yes, Mum. Quite so!" I nodded my answer. "Please, then."

When he realized I was unable to sit up to drink, he reached under my back on the bed and scooped me into a sitting position to take a few sips of orange juice. A little rest in between, and then more sips, until I started to feel myself coming back into a slightly more solid physical state of being. When my words recovered a bit, I thanked him repeatedly and, then, brightening as though I had suddenly had a marvellous idea, said, "Oh! I have a son!"

He nodded. "That's nice, Mum."

I blurted out, "No! I mean I have a son! Here! In this hotel!"

After what seemed endless queries from my Irish lad, I was finally able to give him my son's name. He dialled up Jason's room and told him, "You best come to your mother's room. I think she needs you here."

I passed out again for a bit and awoke to find Jason sitting beside my bed. The two young men were watching me, and then they began to feed me more juice. I remember Jason thanking the night clerk and staying close by me until the breakfast service was available in the morning. We dressed and went down to have some proper food.

It became evident over the next hours that I had likely had a stroke or at least some form of brain damage during my "adventure" and had been very close to death's door. At the same time, I had been given quite a miraculous gift that I will treasure until my time comes to leave this life. The gift of choice. Gratitude saturates me.

I was travelling with a number of gifted spiritual and other therapeutic healers, and chose to stay with the bus rather than seek orthodox medical attention in a foreign country. Gradually recovering speech and most of my balance in the next few days and weeks, I hold the whole experience as a beautiful teaching and a true Irish blessing.

HAZELWOOD

Deep in the Hazelwood
Spring water trickling
Magic delivered from soil to soul
Drink deeply, as broken parts
Transform to whole.

Stories well-woven
and shared, free for listening
Wet rocks all glistening
as wonders unfold.

Men of hard farm labours
One with the land
Invite us to notice
the Mysteries at hand.

A WALK ACROSS THE BOURNE

Have you ever looked at your skin under a microscope? It's a landscape of patterning and cross-patterning, like the irregular criss cross of cracked lava that forms in the upper crust of a volcanic crater. Such is the floor of the expanse of valley that is the Bourne.

Surrounded by high ridges on three sides and the sea on the fourth, it is a world of wonders unto itself. At the foot of the ridge, along the far side, is a thick Hazelwood, which offers springs of water, clear and fresh tasting, with healing properties for the wholeness of body and soul.

In the myriad cracks between the rocks that make up the floor of the valley, there grows an embarrassment of riches in terms of the many genus and cultivars of plant life. These include plants of many climates, since the different depths and widths of cracks provide a variety of microclimatic conditions for plant growth. Every type of plant, from tropical to the high mountain Edelweiss of the alps, grows in these cracks.

At the gateway where the bus dropped us off, there was a collection of walking sticks cut from local tree branches for us to choose from. We were met by our guide, Pat (of course), who led us across the valley a couple of miles out toward the Hazelwood. As we went along, he pointed out and discussed the botanical surprises along the way.

Pat looked an awful lot like my mom's cousin George, which is only appropriate due to my maternal Irish heritage, I suppose. Partway across, we saw a lone figure coming toward us from a different area of the valley. This man was not only a local farmer and a good friend of Pat's, he was also known to be a man of magic and wisdom. A storyteller and a seer.

A bit big for a leprechaun, he stood about six-feet two-inches tall, with the square-shouldered, broad-handed build of a farmer. Somehow, though, I felt he carried a sense of clarity and even a touch of vulnerability about him.

I had been told previously on this trip, by others with intuition and vision, to watch out for a James or a Jim, for that one would have something to tell me. When Pat introduced this new companion to our walk as Jim, I was immediately alerted to his possible teaching. As soon as I got the opportunity to speak to Jim, I told him of those predictions.

He grinned and said, "Oh, you were told that were you? Well, we'll see if we don't get a chance out here for a wee talk then."

We all moved on with our walking tour of the valley and eventually reached the Hazelwood. Jim then regaled us with the magical stories of the Hazelwood and the fairies that danced about in the forest near the beautiful freshwater springs. Many of our group took a drink from the spring and then moved up the hill for a look at a nearby cave.

My legs were still a bit wobbly and my balance a bit off from the adventures the night of my blessing in the hotel, so I stayed behind. It gave me and Jim a chance to talk together.

"Well, let's see what the Maker wants me to tell you," said Jim, with a long pause while he put his hand on my shoulder like a blessing. He then went into a deeper mindfulness. He told me that I'd be all right, that my legs needed to be taken care of thoroughly when any wound came along, that I must be vigilant, and the rest would be okay also, provided I didn't let the discouragers dampen my spirit. He told me a bit about what he felt was important for me to know about my health on several levels.

As he spoke, my state of mind deepened, similar to when I am acting as a conduit for Reiki healing, and I could feel the delicacy of this big man's heart at the same time as its high integrity. When we finished, I looked up at him with great respect, and we shared a moment of mutual recognition before the rest of the gang returned from their visit to the caves on the hill. We then walked back across the valley to the bus. A couple of our group spoke with Jim along the way, and then at some point he left us to head off from whence he came.

We finally reached the bus. Lots of hugs and hearty handshakes later, we left Pat and the Bourne behind, and headed off to our next destination, most of us quietly contemplating all we had seen, heard, and felt.

Less than two weeks later, I heard from our trip leaders, Denise and Gerry, that Jim Monahan had passed away. Yes, my heart replied. He already had the angel dust on him.

WALKING WITH JOY

This Entity that walks with me
when **JOY** directs me here
Is quiet, yet a symphony,
Sweet music to my ear

I feel I know what Grandma meant
by her "Blessed Assurance"
My Ally, steady, walks with me
Through every Life occurrence

Not a god of distant form,
Nor man's denominations
This Ally speaks no rules for me
Nor fear, nor limitations

We simply move, together
Through what is ours to do
This Entity sustains me
It brings me here to you

I wonder what your note is
That will sound within my song
I trust her sense of harmony
JOY would never lead me wrong

GRECIAN TRAVELS

Twice, now, I have travelled to Greece on a tour led by my dear friend and teacher, Jean Houston. Each of these visits has been unique unto itself. Even those particularly essential sites worthy of visiting on both occasions were so rich with history and story that there was plenty to be learned and enjoyed on more than one visit.

We, as a troop of soul explorers, were treated to the finest of collections of antiquities in the generous number of temples and sacred sites. We ate only the most delicious of Greek foods and stayed in the most interesting and comfortable accommodations. We explored the grounds of the ancient Olympian stadiums, Athenian and other temples, and flora and fauna native to Greece. We swam in the Aegean Sea, rode ferries from one Greek island to another. We were simply IMMERSED in the GREEKNESS of it all.

One of our trips was taken a mere two weeks after my Irish blessing. I phoned Jean to explain to her what I'd been through and asked her guidance as to whether I should join the group in Greece as originally planned. (I did not want to slow down the various climbs and walks with my compromised sense of balance.)

She simply said, "You MUST come!"

I am so very glad that I did! One of my favourite spots in Greece is the Temple of Poseidon on a high rocky cliff rising at the edge of the Aegean Sea. The last few days of our journey were spent at a beautiful hotel within sight of that magnificent temple.

One day, the whole group visited and admired the temple with its tall, elegant columns and distinctive markings, such as the one left behind many years ago by Lord Byron on a visit to the site.

Just down the cliff, below the temple, there is a kind of courtyard with a few square, carved stones, big enough and flat enough to sit on while losing oneself in contemplation of the energy and mythology of the place.

After a talk with us about the stories of Poseidon, Jean had descended to this courtyard to sit for a while on one of the stones, evidently deep in her own thoughts. I went down and sat on the next rock to hers. I had no desire to interrupt her reverie and yet was drawn to be nearby.

After a time, she glanced up at me and waved me over to sit beside her. Jean then shared with me a visual gift that still holds its purpose for me when I am feeling challenged to keep it together in my day-to-day life. One of the images used to represent Poseidon in tales written and illustrated for the enjoyment of children is the octopus. Picture if you will, an octopus with the crown and royal bearing of the God of the Waves.

Jean gestured out to the sea all around us as she described him to me. Then she pointed out the generous blocks of stone and pieces of column that at some point in history seemed to have tumbled down the cliff and were strewn randomly over the slope. The suggestion for me was to solicit the help of Poseidon when I felt, on any level, broken to pieces by circumstances of my life. Poseidon would help me lift those pieces of rock and reassemble them to form a sturdy, stable column of strength to put right any disorder in my perceptions and circumstances. This image has indeed stayed with me in times of need.

I am blessed with a deep respect and love of the power and the creatures of the sea.

[Cinder celebrated her 60th birthday
in GREECE, 2015]

SWIMMING CIRCLES AROUND ME

On another journey with Jean and fellow explorers within her community, I was thrilled to spend some time on the big island of Hawaii. It was not my first visit to Hawaii, having lived there one winter with my family when I was nine years old. So much has changed over the decades since then, and yet the soul of the place remains so familiar.

We had a marvellous time experiencing the culture and mythology, the food and flora of the island. Volcanoes impressed us, the ocean embraced us, and the breezes soothed our souls. We were instructed in the basics of Hula dance, the making of grass braids, and the making of leis. We even donned most of the clothes in our suitcases to survive the freezing temperatures at the mountaintops where the observatories were keeping watch on the galaxy beyond us.

One day, we were left to our own devices while our Jean was busy with a project doing some video recording on the island. About a dozen of us decided to take a boat ride to see the dolphins.

We boarded a boat at a nearby dock, with a captain and two crew (both female), and replete with snorkelling equipment and a packed lunch. We set off into the Pacific waters well off shore.

We rode the waves and gentle swells out about 4.5 miles from the shoreline to reach an area where pods of dolphins had been reported. Arriving at the designated coordinates, the skipper stopped the forward movement, and we all watched to see whether anyone could see any pods. The crew told us their depth-finders had picked up on what they believed we were looking for just near the back of the boat.

We all set about donning our snorkel gear—masks, breathing tubes, and flippers—and most began lowering themselves into the water off the platform on the boat's aft quarter.

I was slower than most, trying to be careful with the flippers so as not to reinjure the sole of my right foot. When I was finally ready, I looked around and saw that I was the only one left on the deck.

For a moment, I watched the small crowd splashing and giggling excitedly in the water beyond the boat. The thought crossed my mind, *No dolphin in his right mind is going to go near THAT!*

I looked up at the skipper perched in his pilot seat on the highest deck of the boat. By use of sign language and a lot of begging and pointing motions, I sought his permission to go into the water in the opposite direction from the rest of the swimmers. He was not going to allow it at first. Eventually though, he signalled he would keep an eye on me from where he was and to go ahead. I was very happy to be slipping into the ocean on my own and began to sing a little song (from Raffi) as I went into the water:

```
"Baby Beluga in the Big Blue Sea
Swims so Wild and he Swims so Free
Heaven's above and the sea's below
He's a little White Whale on the Go"
```

I gently pushed away from the hull of the boat and fluttered ever-so-gently my flippers and hands until I was probably about 40 feet from the boat itself, where I just tried to maintain position ... still singing my little song. I was becoming aware of a sense of "not being alone."

A ripple of silver-grey passed beneath me, and then again the other way. *Was that a dolphin?* I wondered. Then it happened again. This time I heard squeaks and other vocal noises that assured me I was indeed in the presence of dolphins!

Oh, boy! I thought happily. *My favourite!* Cautiously moving my face just a bit, I realized I was actually SURROUNDED by dolphins! They swam in a circle around me, swimming two-by-two, counter-clockwise. There must have been about 40 of them or more!

Listening to their sounds, the squeaks and clicks, I tried my best to imitate them. They seemed to be really interested in this and made even more, different sounds. I kept trying to imitate them, doing a pretty lousy job of it, if I do say so myself!

Then I began singing my little song again. I wondered if they'd give it a try, but they just kept swimming around me while I sang to them. I was afloat in a sense of peace and safety such as I have never felt before ... on land or in water!

Then the thought came into my mind that I'd better see where the boat was. I had been so wrapped up in my play with the dolphins that I hadn't looked up in a while. I said good-bye to my dolphin friends and rose my head above water to take a look. The boat was about twice as far as I expected, so I began to swim with purpose toward it. (That's with PURPOSE, not "Porpoise," hee hee.)

When I reached the boat, I realized that most of the group were already back on board and the skipper was giving me a scolding finger waggle.

"You went too far from the boat!" he scolded. "We ARE five miles from the shore, you know!" But when he saw the big smile on my face that even his stern words could not erase, his expression gentled a bit. "How was it?" he asked.

I just grinned and said, "WOW!"

"I've only ever seen that happen in one other circumstance," he said. "When the whales come to this area from the further ocean to have their babies, the dolphins circle them like that and protect both the mama whale and the babies until they get oriented to swimming close together with their mamas in the water."

I put my hands on my hips and challenged him. "Are you saying I look like a WHALE??"

He laughed and put his hands up in a defensive position. "NO! No! A BABY whale!!"

TIMELESS TIME

As I consider, here, some of the pearls I have had the privilege to gather along the way, I cannot help but notice how many I have let alone, still waiting for their moment to serve, to be appreciated in the recognition of my life's blessings.

Not all pearls are beautiful at first sight. Some are. Some pearls are immediately shiny, like little beacons of light, dancing around in the reflection of Grace. Something as simple and profound as a smile. Other pearls are wrapped in a disguise of pain, or fear, or the horrid alchemy of both combined. Nevertheless, they too are pearls. In time, perhaps most keenly in the experience of timeless time, they are revealed. What can seem like an endless unyielding string between the pearls turns out to be the most valuable treasures after all.

One way or another, I have come to believe that of every situation we face, at least every one that we face with love and the willingness to learn,we can lean on our Beloved of the Soul to walk through with us. Our experiences are all jewels waiting to be revealed in their own due time.

I hope that you have enjoyed these pearls I've shared through my stories and poems. Even more, my wish for you is that your life's pearls take on a lustre of

their own as you consider them for the great teach-
ers and treasures they can be. I wish you pearls, and
even more … I wish you JOY.

FLIGHT WITH JOY

Joy!
Oh Glorious Joy
You're here!
Like gull on silver wing
you soar and reel
a flash of light
against the clouds,
you squeal and cry
and sheer carefree abandon
steers your course.
Oh carry me
uplift me
higher, higher
like a child
who laughs with gleeful panic
in a giddy, heady
freefall on the
rollercoaster sky.
We fly, Joy and I,
and Oh! the wondrous view
we see below us
as we take our place
in this the moving picture
God has made,
and has invited us
to decorate
with all the beauty of our souls.
Fly! FLY!
Fly!!

EPILOGUE

A day or two after I completed the writing of this book, I had a download from my higher self and decided to call it:

CINDER'S CREED

TODAY

TODAY I PULL MY HEAD OUT OF
THAT LONG DARK TUNNEL
WHERE THE SUN DON'T SHINE.

TODAY, I QUIT FOCUSING ON THE
BEST WAY TO DIE
AND TURN MY THOUGHTS AND MIND
TO THE BEST WAY TO LIVE.

TODAY IS A DAY OF CREATIVITY
DEVELOPING JOY
REJECTING DEFEAT
GROWING ASSURANCE
AND SENSIBLE COMPASSION.

TODAY, I RECOGNIZE
THE GIFTS I HAVE BEEN GIVEN
AND SET ABOUT GROWING THEM
INTO GIFTS FOR THE WORLD AROUND ME.

TODAY IS THE DAY FOR RE-BIRTH.
IN THE WORDS OF A SKILLED COACH
"BE A FAUCET ... NOT A DRAIN!"

SO BE IT.

CINDER

Printed in Canada